The Responsible Object

The Responsible Object
A History of Design Ideology for the Future

Marjanne van Helvert (ed.)

With contributions by
Andrea Bandoni
Ece Canlı
Alison J. Clarke
Éva Forgács
Marjanne van Helvert
Susan R. Henderson
Ed van Hinte
Elizabeth Carolyn Miller
Luiza Prado de O. Martins &
Pedro J. S. Vieira de Oliveira

Valiz, Amsterdam
Ueberschwarz, Melbourne

Contents

ARCHAE-OLOGISTS THINK OF OUR TIME?

Introduction
A History of Design for the Future

Marjanne van Helvert

What would future archaeologists think of our time, if they were to dig in the places that used to house our long gone civilization? Operating from some dystopian, post-apocalyptic 'desert of the real', full of menacing artificial intelligence, zombies, or post-human humanoids, or alternatively from the green, clean, utopian oasis of a more optimistic future, they would certainly have no trouble finding stuff. Once, the only physical leftovers of forgotten times were bones, stones, and later metal pieces, all of the more perishable materials such as wood and textiles having long since decomposed. Digging for treasure from the twentieth century, however, would result in the discovery of countless dumpsites of things we threw away: plastic and metal objects, still smouldering heaps of discarded electronics, synthetic textiles, and other things that do not decompose within a foreseeable passage of time. Then there would be the boneyards of automobiles, ships, and aircraft that have accumulated over the past century, and perhaps there will be ruins of abandoned cities and shopping malls full of crumbling concrete and asphalt. What the archaeologists of the future would find are the leftovers of an age of rampant, imperishable, man-made objects.

Today, in an economic system that revolves around producing and consuming these objects, we are starting to review their role in a series of challenges that lie ahead of us. Through global warming and environmental pollution we have been transforming essential life-sustaining systems on our planet on such a scale that a dramatic impact on the quality of life of future generations is unavoidable. In reaction to the growing awareness of these issues, some designers are taking responsibility for developing more sustainable products and systems, and for promoting a more equitable distribution of resources that might allow for everyone to benefit equally from increasingly necessary strate-

Marjanne van Helvert

gies to cope with climate change, loss of biodiversity and material scarcity. Within the design discipline, sustainability and social responsibility have become some of the most prolific buzzwords of the past decade, generating countless new products, materials, and technological implementations, as well as books, exhibitions, and conferences on these subjects.[1] Often grouped together under popular adjectives such as sustainable, green, eco, humanitarian, critical, and, most encompassing, social design, they represent a new wave of socially committed design that expresses itself in objects and concepts designed to improve people's present-day lives and futures, and products and initiatives that endeavour to change the world.

Despite the focus on contemporary issues as new challenges for the design discipline, most of these design problems and solutions are not new. They are not unchartered territory but have been part of the canon of industrial design history, as well as of world-wide, vernacular design traditions. Needless to say, many of the recent social design practices are based on ancient developments and techniques that have proved their merit in the centuries before industrialization. During most of human history, natural materials and renewable energy sources were the only ones available, and recycling and repairing artefacts has always been indispensable considering their material value, as it still is for many people all over the world. These practices are now being reinvented and adapted for a new age and are transformed through new production and communication technologies. Many examples of what we call social design also, though perhaps unconsciously, build on western traditions of idealistic, ideological, utopian, sometimes noble-minded and sometimes quite patronizing or even neocolonial design solutions of the past century or so. Quite often present-day design concepts

1
For some examples of such books, see 'Bibliography', p. 270.

reproduce ideas that have appeared several times before in the history of design, and are, for example, reminiscent of the ideals of the Arts and Crafts movement, of the techno-optimism of the space age, or the humanitarian design of the 1970s. It is good to be aware of this history, to take note of the successes of the past, and of possible pitfalls of seemingly simple solutions. Furthermore, there may be interesting designs, attempts, and ideas that run the risk of being forgotten, because they were not considered relevant at the time or were not as spectacular or aesthetically pleasing as their contemporaries that did end up in the history books.

Any recorded history not only reflects the values, ideals, politics, and preferences of the past but also those of the time in which it was written. As we presently live in a world dominated by capitalism, the design canon generally emphasizes the designers and designs that fit capitalist ideals, such as wealth, growth, innovation, and status. Yet there are key moments in history when design was dominated by socialist and environmentalist narratives and ideals, such as emancipation, equality, durability, and ecology. This book gathers a number of examples of designers and movements from the past century and a half that combined ethical and aesthetical ideals, with the idea of changing the world for the better through their designs. Long before the long-term effects of unbridled industrialization and consumption became as clear as they are today, these designers were already concerned about disposability, waste, and toxins, and about the grossly unequal distribution of resources and rights, both locally and globally. They thought about what design could do to improve the durability, functionality, and availability of products, as well as improve the circumstances under which they are made, and the well-being of their users.

Marjanne van Helvert

This book presents a selected history of socially committed design within the Western design tradition since early modernism. It is therefore limited, as is any design history that only looks at Western traditions, to a small group of mostly white, mostly upper- or middle-class, mostly male, mostly educated, mostly professional persons. This necessarily means it excludes, as design history conventionally has done, the achievements of women, minorities, non-Western practitioners, amateurs, and other groups and individuals that have not been considered part of the industrial design canon. A history of socially committed design from a wider, more inclusive perspective would be invaluable and much needed as well,[2] yet in this book the choice has been made to focus on the intersection of design and consumer society in the history of the industrialized world. Many of our biggest challenges appear to be heavily embedded in our current system of industrial production and consumption of designed and manufactured goods, and it is time for a reconsideration of what that same design tradition has put forward to alter and subvert this system. Moreover, to avoid framing social design as something that exists only outside of mainstream design, as something separate that can easily be ignored, it is important to call attention to socially committed practices within conventional design history as well. The following chapters offer a chronological selection of designers and design movements whose ideals, dilemmas, and designed solutions show significant parallels with those of designers today. Some of them have long been part of the Western industrial design canon, while others are perhaps less well-known. The subjects have also been selected to represent recurring themes within socially committed design practices and theories, such as craftsmanship, techno-optimism, scarcity, labour conditions, repair,

2
Luckily, one such history is being written. Architect and researcher Vibhavari Jani is currently, at the time of completion of this book, editing a volume on non-Western sustainable design and architecture. She has previously published *Diversity in Design: Perspectives from the Non-Western World* (New York: Fairchild Books, 2011).

recycling, renewable materials, mass production, consumerism, counterculture, modernism, postmodernism, obsolescence, humanitarianism, and ecology.

William Morris (1834–1896) and the Arts and Crafts movement appear in the first chapter of many design histories, as they can be seen to represent the beginning of product design as an independently recognized discipline, and were highly influential in the development of early modern design in the late nineteenth and early twentieth century. Arts and Crafts was in part an attempt at reconfiguring the role of design and craftsmanship within a newly industrialized society. Morris was one of the fiercest critics of mass production, and his preference for craftsmanship over industrial production has recently led to comparisons with the current craft revival and the maker movement.[3] Despite being a passionate socialist, Morris worked almost exclusively for a wealthy elite, as his hand-crafted, durable products were not affordable to the average consumer, which is a dilemma that many designers today recognize. In her contribution, Elizabeth Carolyn Miller focuses on one of the ventures of Morris's later career, the Kelmscott Press (1891–1896), which published and produced exclusive books, and allowed Morris to put many of his ideals into practice. His visions are perhaps most inspiringly realized within the fictional setting of his utopian novel News from Nowhere (1890), which describes an ideal society having overcome all of our social, environmental, and design problems, most of which are as relevant today as they were then.

Arts and Crafts ideas were adopted and advanced throughout Europe and North America in the early twentieth century, and were further developed through design organizations such as the Wiener Werkstätte and the Deutscher Werkbund. A next big step in the relation between design and industry was taken by the

3
See for example: Evgeny Morozov, 'Making It', The New Yorker 13 January 2014, www.newyorker.com/magazine/2014/01/13/making-it-2 (accessed 12 May 2016).

Marjanne van Helvert

Bauhaus (1919–1932). In what was perhaps the most famous design school in history, the goal was set at bringing industry, design, and craftsmanship together in an effort to make good design available to everybody. At the same time in post-revolutionary Russia, a design school called VKhUTEMAS (1920–1930) was founded with quite similar ambitions, yet in a completely different political setting. Éva Forgács recounts how both schools evolved their revolutionary influential design principles amidst tempestuous social changes and material scarcity.

Margarete Schütte-Lihotzky, (1897–2000) was another decidedly left-wing designer and architect. Although forgotten and virtually erased from history for almost half a century, today she is most recognized for her Frankfurt kitchen of 1927, a milestone in modern, standardized kitchen design. With her progressive vision she designed apartments for single women, schools, nurseries, and modular and built-in furniture, and went to Soviet Russia to help design whole new cities in the 1930s. Susan R. Henderson describes how not only Lihotzky's impressive career has been largely ignored because she was a woman, and a communist with many of her works in Eastern Europe and Russia destroyed in the Second World War, but also that she was exemplary of the type of designer that always put her political ideals first and mostly worked on the design of the everyday.

During and after the Second World War, many countries were confronted with material scarcity. To prevent a rampant price increase of products such as furniture, crockery and textiles, some governments developed elaborate schemes in order to counter shortages and ensure the availability of affordable, good quality products. The British CC41 Utility clothing scheme was in effect from 1941 to 1949 and employed high profile designers in an attempt to not only provide sufficient goods at reasonable prices, but also to promote modern, functionalist design to all citizens. It provides an interesting case study on the effects of designing with the idea of using the least amount of raw material and as little labour as possible, as well as on a systematic redistribution of scarce resources in order to ensure equality in times of crisis, in which the burden always rests heavier on the shoulders of the economically deprived. The attempted democratization of what was considered good design continued in post-war Europe and in the US as well, and this promotion of modern taste had a lasting effect on the design discipline.

The post-war economic boom in North America and later in Western Europe fostered a growing middle class, and lowered the prices of commodities through increased mass production. Consumer society was flourishing, and designers became stars of modern living, creating design icons that hold their status to this day. Industrial designers were assigned the task of plugging into commercial success and increase product turnover by employing styling and other forms of designed obsolescence. These techniques soon came under fire because of their implications of disposability and waste. Much of the concerns about overproduction, low-quality products, fast fashion, and planned obsolescence that we hear today were already voiced loudly in the 1950s and 1960s.

A different voice and one quite dominant in the design discipline today is that of the techno-utopian, arguably fathered by Richard Buckminster Fuller (1895–1983). After going through an existential crisis in his early thirties, Fuller, according to himself, decided to dedicate his life to changing the world and improving the condition of all humanity. In his contribution, Ed van Hinte recounts how Fuller invented, or re-invented,

Marjanne van Helvert

principles for efficient and lightweight constructions that save material and energy, and how he created such iconic structures as the geodesic dome and the aluminium, prefab Dymaxion House. He also popularized the term 'spaceship earth', which is the idea of regarding our planet as an independent vessel in space with ultimately finite resources. Fuller's unconventional inventions went on to influence a range of counterculture and experimental designers in the second half of the twentieth century, and both his designs and his ideas remain visible inspirations to this day.

One of the most vocal critics from within the design discipline has been Victor Papanek (1923–1998). He argued that designers seemed to have gotten lost in creating useless and even dangerous objects, while their skills would be so much more useful in areas that design had neglected. Papanek is one of the main protagonists of the humanitarian design movement of the 1970s, of which much of today's social design can be seen as an extension. Alison J. Clarke provides insight into Papanek's ideas and how they were received in the established design community. He was not only uncompromisingly committed to the social responsibility of design, but also very concerned about the role of designers in environmental issues. Going against mainstream principles, Papanek did not believe in the workings of copyrights and patents and often published his designs for free to be copied and used by anyone.

While some designers worked decidedly from political conviction, or were persuaded by the spirit of the age, others went downright against the grain. The work of William Morris, Margarete Schütte-Lihotzky and many people from Bauhaus and VKhUTEMAS was highly influenced by the political changes happening around them, this being a time of massive social housing projects and working class emancipation in many industrialized countries, which provided important state commissions to architects and designers. Victor Papanek and many other socially committed designers in the second half of the twentieth century found themselves, purposely or not, in a more countercultural position. Design had come to be recognized as a mature and influential discipline and was thoroughly internalized by the commercial industry. The counterculture movement of the 1960s and 1970s, spreading from North America to much of the Western world, proved, paradoxically perhaps, a testament to the success of consumer capitalist society, as the latter quickly appropriated the aesthetics and values of youth culture and of alternative social and cultural movements as marketable strategies. After several decades of predominantly modernist design, a plethora of pop culture influences took over. At the same time, hippies and back-to-the-landers in the US experimented with alternative ways of building and living, in a pragmatic attempt to construct DIY utopia outside of mainstream society. In Europe, the conceptual designers of the Radical or Anti-Design movement dealt utopian modernism its final, hyperbolic blow with their megalomaniac, dystopian visions of future urban structures. In the postmodern era that followed, which lasted roughly two or three decades, political content was highly subverted by irony and pastiche. Humanitarian and ecodesign continued to exist in the margins, but the star designers of the economically booming 1980s and 1990s were not primarily known for their social responsibility or environmental awareness. It was not until the multiple crises of the early years of the new millennium that the search for responsible design resurfaced in its current shape and scale.

The final three chapters in this book offer a glance at possible futures of socially committed design, con-

Marjanne van Helvert

ceptualized today. Ece Canlı offers a perspective on queer design culture, recounting how oppressed minorities and identities are slowly gaining visibility within the historically uniformly white, male design discipline and within culture and society as a whole. Starting from feminist design practices in the past, she proposes queer theory as an inclusive and subversive strategy for resisting discriminatory norms and values within design. In the following chapter, Andrea Bandoni analyses the presently much hyped maker movement from the perspective of a series of newly installed fabrication laboratories (fab labs) in economically deprived areas in Brazil. The publicly available technologies of fab labs are meant to emancipate citizens to design, customize, and produce artefacts themselves, and have inspired some to proclaim a third industrial revolution based on decentralized production that could yield a more equal and sustainable society. Finally, Luiza Prado de O. Martins and Pedro J. S. Vieira de Oliveira conclude with a speculative vision on the potential dangers of some social design projects, reminding us that design is always political.

Today, a rather technocratic approach dominates social and sustainable design, as it does the design field at large, in which problem solving does not seem to require any active political awareness, and designing as an activity is attributed with a kind of transcendental quality. The ideology that speaks from many examples of socially committed design today is one that is based on the belief in the power of design and technology as the determining forces in solving the most challenging issues before us. 'Design thinking' is being promoted in countless possible situations, fields and professions. It assumes that designers possess unique and universal problem solving skills which can offer creative solutions in any discipline.[4] Designers are being asked by

4
For more on design thinking, see for example: Richard Buchanan, 'Wicked Problems in Design Thinking', *Design Issues* 8, no. 2 (Spring 1992), pp. 5–21.

governments and corporations to brainstorm about 'wicked problems' such as terrorism, climate change, or unemployment. In such instances, the derived solutions often only target symptoms rather than confront the complex problems themselves, as that would require a long-term immersion into the social, economic, historical, geographical, political, and many other sides of the problem. Historically, designers have largely worked in service of the minority of the richest people on the planet. They have, so far, not deployed their talents and skills on a similar scale to turn around such pervasive issues as institutionalized socio-economic inequality or climate change. Wherever considerable strides forward have been made—such as in the case of halting the dwindling of the ozone layer in the 1990s or, further back in time, lifting up millions of working class citizens in European cities out of the poverty and hopelessness of slums—it was surely not without the help of political legislation and social change.

However, if design in itself is not the solution, it will certainly be part of any solution, in much the same way as it is also part of the problem. Design is always influenced by its social and political context, and by the cultural assumptions and history of the designer, the client, and consumer. It is shaped by all of our values and desires, and in turn it is always in the process of confirming, evolving, or, less commonly, subverting the way we live, eat, move, look, communicate, work and play.[5] Therefore all design is laden with political ideals, whether they are purposely bestowed on it or carried unconsciously. Despite the ambitions of the modernists, it can never be universal, neutral, or innocent, and is on the contrary often concerned with promoting some values over others. Wherever design is employed as a solution to a problem, politics are irrevocably involved, be it in the choice and formulation of the

5
As design theorists Dunne and Raby have termed it, there is either 'affirmative' or 'critical' design. Anthony Dunne and Fiona Raby, *Design Noir: The Secret Life of Electronic Objects* (Basel, Boston and Berlin: Birkhäuser 2001), p. 58.

Marjanne van Helvert

WEALTHIER PEOPLE CAN

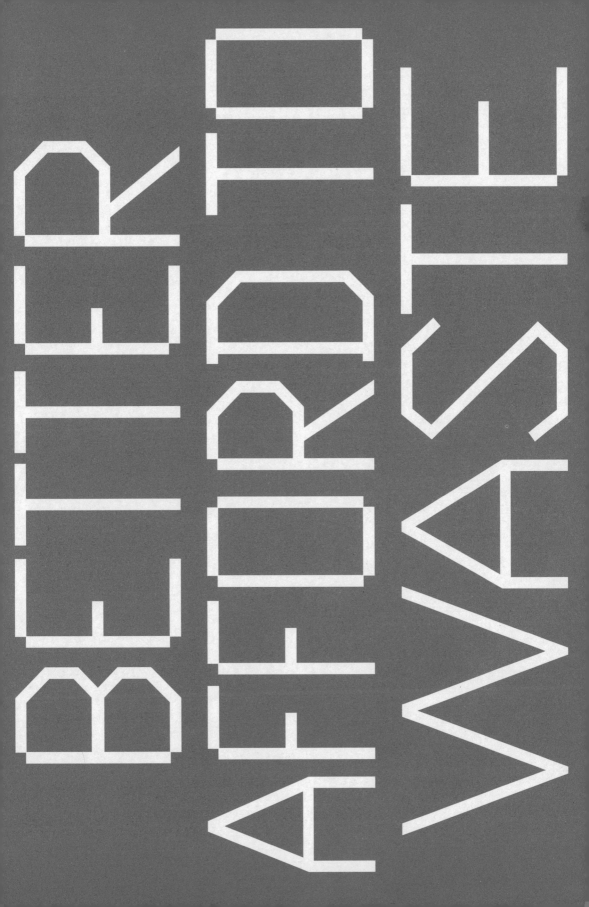

problem, or the aesthetical, productional, and material values in the designed solution. We have to see design as something that is never above ideology, but instead needs a stronger political awareness if it is to constructively move forward on complex social and environmental issues.

Design theory and design history are relatively young fields of research. They have only recently started to become recognized as serious academic disciplines, and there is still a large gap between the worlds of design practitioners and design theorists. Unlike architecture, which has a long-standing, profound, and widely valued academic tradition, design does not yet fully profit from theoretical foundations and critical, historical analysis. Because of its urgent nature, the field of socially committed design would benefit considerably from a more widespread historical awareness and more developed critical theory. This is therefore not another book about social or sustainable design today. This is a book about learning from its rich history, so that we are better prepared for the future. It is about designers who have dedicated their lives to changing the world, and about confrontations between ideals and reality. It is about revolutionary failures and invaluable steps forward. It is simultaneously a critique and above all a celebration of the tireless spirit of idealism and creativity.

William Morris, Arts and Crafts, and the Idea of Eco-Socialist Design

Elizabeth Carolyn Miller

1

See especially Ruskin's 'The Nature of Gothic'. For more on the influence of Ruskin's expressive theory of labour, see Tim Barringer, *Men at Work: Art and Labour in Victorian Britain* (New Haven: Yale University Press, 2005).

2

Printing chintzes at Merton Abbey, Morris & Co.'s Textile Workshop, c. 1890.

3

I take 'seamless' from Peter Stansky, *Redesigning the World: William Morris, the 1880s, and the Arts and Crafts* (Princeton: Princeton University Press, 1985, rpt. Palo Alto: Society for the Promotion of Science and Scholarship, 1996), p. 7.

William Morris, a leader in the Arts and Crafts movement and a forbearer of modern theorists of sustainable design, inherited from John Ruskin the idea of labour as a form of artistic expression that is vital to human dignity. Ruskin and Morris believed that a trace of the worker's craft should be present in all responsibly created objects.[1] Working in the second half of the nineteenth century, Morris voiced an early disgust for industrial capitalism and its effects on labour, production, and art. These convictions persisted throughout his career, from the initial launch of his design firm Morris, Marshall, Faulkner & Co. in 1861, which was succeeded by Morris & Co. in 1875,[2] to his conversion to socialism in the early 1880s, which led him to spend the final years of his life campaigning for the socialist cause. If Ruskin was the leading light in Morris's early revival of handcraft methods, Marx was equally influential on his later work, but Morris's politics and aesthetics remained closely knit together throughout his career, seamless within his evolving beliefs.[3]

Morris's design ideology was central to his vision of socialism and his vision of a more just society, and while his ideas of production have received more attention than his ideas of consumption, both were fundamental to his notion of the responsible object. Critics have sometimes viewed Morris's late career as hypocritical, since he continued to pioneer expensive hand production while openly denouncing luxury and economic inequality on the socialist platform, but by focusing on Morris's ideas about waste and consumption, we can see how his work foreshadows contemporary theories of sustainable design. His emphasis on durability, his passion for preservation, and his respect for materials were all fundamental to his idea of the responsible object. By focusing on his turn to book design in the 1890s, we can see how Morris brought his socialist ideals into design practice.

Elizabeth Carolyn Miller

Morris spent the 1880s deeply immersed in socialist propaganda: editing the Socialist League's newspaper *Commonweal*,[4] and maintaining an intensely demanding schedule of political meetings, lectures, and debates. As Florence Boos notes in her introduction to Morris's socialist diary of 1887, 'Morris's achievements routinely exhaust the enumerative abilities of his biographers'. (The diary itself, indeed, had to be given up after three months, due to Morris's pressing public commitments.[5]) But from 1891 until his death in 1896, Morris embarked on a new design venture that many have viewed as a departure from this intense political work: the Kelmscott Press.[6] Kelmscott pioneered the fine press movement, and it came to produce the most expensive and exclusive books of its day. These lavishly decorated, handmade editions included the *Kelmscott Chaucer*,[7] which was the press's largest, grandest, and costliest book. When published in 1896, it sold for the steep price of £20 (£33 if bound in pigskin) and its limited edition printing of 425 copies sold out before the work was finished. Thirteen additional copies printed on vellum sold for the even more exorbitant price of 120 guineas (approximately £125). The 'paradox of price' has been a longstanding puzzle for those interested in the social implications of Morris's design work for Morris & Co., but it is an even more pressing problem with respect to the Kelmscott Press, given Morris's active engagement in socialism by this time.[8] No other Kelmscott books were as expensive as the Chaucer, but many were priced by the guinea (worth 21 shillings) rather than the pound, and while the use of this currency measurement fit with the press's neo-medieval aesthetic and tendency toward archaic language, the guinea was strongly associated with luxury consump-

4

Cover of the *Commonweal*, 1890.

5
William Morris, *Socialist Diary*, ed. Florence Boos (Iowa City: Windhover Press, 1981).

6

William Morris, Kelmscott Press logo, 1891.

7

The Works of Geoffrey Chaucer now newly imprinted (London: Kelmscott Press, 1896).

8
'Paradox of price' is Stansky's term (p. 47–48).

9
The guinea coin (worth 21 shillings) was no longer minted after 1813, but continued to be used as a currency measurement associated with luxury goods and with the professions rather than the trades. See Sally Mitchell, *Daily Life in Victorian England* (Westport: Greenwood, 1996), p. 31.

10
Quoted in Colin Clair, *A History of Printing in Britain* (London: Cassell, 1965), p. 246.

tion and also evoked the class distinction between 'trade' and 'profession' that Arts and Crafts purportedly opposed through its respect for the status of skilled labour.[9] Even the most evidently socialist of the Kelmscott books were priced by the guinea, such as the 1892 Kelmscott edition of Morris's socialist utopian novel *News from Nowhere*, priced at 2 guineas for its 300 paper copies and 10 guineas for its 10 vellum copies.

The Kelmscott Press was particularly prone to accusations of hypocrisy because it made books, and unlike other commodities books were thought to have an enlightening or liberating potential for the newly literate working classes. As Arthur Pendenys wrote in an open letter to Morris: 'If you were consistent your Printing Press would exist for the sake of spreading knowledge. As it is your publications appeal to capitalists and others of the wealthy classes.'[10] Thorstein Veblen, an early theorist of capitalism who coined the term 'conspicuous consumption', likewise criticized the Kelmscott Press in his 1899 book *Theory of the Leisure Class*. He called the Press a prime example of the 'conspicuous waste' that characterizes modern forms of consumption:

> These products, since they require hand labour, are more expensive; they are also less convenient for use...; they therefore argue ability on the part of the purchaser to consume freely, as well as ability to waste time and effort. ... The Kelmscott Press reduced the matter to an absurdity ... by issuing books for modern use, edited with the obsolete spelling, printed in black-letter, and bound in limp vellum fitted with thongs.

In handmade paper and hand-bound books, Veblen saw only 'waste', waste that produced nothing except

Elizabeth Carolyn Miller

'pecuniary distinction' for its consumer, and waste that exemplified what Veblen called the 'exaltation of the defective', which Morris had inherited from Ruskin.[11] Veblen insists that his use of the term 'waste' is 'technical' rather than 'deprecatory', but the term is significant in the context of a nascent 'throwaway ethic' or 'culture of disposability' in the late nineteenth century.[12]

11

Thorstein Veblen, *The Theory of the Leisure Class*, 1899 (Harmondsworth, Middlesex: Penguin, 1979), pp. 162–64.

12

Veblen, *Theory*, p. 98. For more on disposability and the 'throwaway culture', see Giles Slade, *Made to Break: Technology and Obsolescence in America* (Cambridge: Harvard University Press, 2006).

Waste, Durability, and Transience

Today, in a moment of acute environmental crisis, the term 'waste' has, of course, taken on a new resonance, one that Veblen did not predict though Morris did. Struggling with the problems of overproduction and superabundance within capitalist society, Morris showed their reliance on a faulty conception of waste, where material goods are imagined to be capable of disappearing without consequence. Threaded through Morris's late career, and perfectly exemplified by the Kelmscott Press, is a counter emphasis on durability and preservation, challenging prevailing notions of waste and offering a distinct theory of the responsible object.

Waste is, of course, strongly correlated with class. Wealthier people can better afford to waste, and as Michael Thompson has described, objects are also classed by their tendency toward waste, so that 'transient' objects are typically low-class while 'antique' or 'durable' objects are high-class.[13] In the historical context of Morris's Kelmscott Press, this meant that cheaply produced Victorian books and periodicals were more accessible to more classes but were fundamentally ephemeral, whereas finely produced books would be less accessible but built to last. The late nineteenth century saw a sharp decline in the price of books and

13

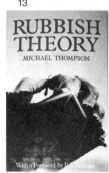

Michael Thompson, *Rubbish Theory: The Creation and Destruction of Value* (Oxford: Oxford University Press, 1979).

periodicals generally, due to new technologies for the mass production of paper and the mechanization of print, and this made for less expensive but also shoddy reading material: the 'ugly' Victorian print that Morris so hated.[14] The 1890s revival of print and the book arts led by Kelmscott Press thus may seem, at first glance, a reaction against the democratization of print, but one need only consider how many of the revival's key figures were socialist or anarchist to doubt such a conclusion: Morris, C.R. Ashbee, T.J. Cobden-Sanderson, and Lucien Pissarro, to name a few.[15] The political affiliations of these men suggest that the fine press movement is better understood, politically, in terms of its stand against capitalist values in production and consumption.

In Morris's conversion story, 'How I Became a Socialist', which ran in the socialist newspaper *Justice* in 1894, Morris attempted to define his idea of socialism, and interestingly the idea of 'waste' figures prominently here:

> Well, what I mean by Socialism is a condition of society in which there should be neither rich nor poor, neither master nor master's man, neither idle nor overworked, neither brain-sick brain workers nor heart-sick hand workers, in a word, in which all men would be living in equality of condition, and would manage their affairs unwastefully.[16]

His socialism is predicated on a key notion of balance: a society with a balanced distribution of goods, he imagines, will be a society without want and without waste. Inequality and wastefulness go hand in hand. This is just one example of what became a major preoccupation in Morris's later career. His 1884 lecture 'Useful Work Versus Useless Toil' employs the word 'waste' eighteen

14
For more on these shifts, see chapters 12-15 of Richard Altick, *The English Common Reader: A Social History of the Mass Reading Public, 1800–1900*, 2nd ed. (Columbus: Ohio State University Press, 1998). For Morris on the Victorian period's 'ugly books', see for example his 1893 lecture 'The Ideal Book' in *The Ideal Book: Essays and Lectures on the Arts of the Book*, ed. William S. Peterson (Berkeley: University of California Press, 1982), p. 67.

15
For more on these presses, see for example Clair, *A History of Printing*; Marcella D. Genz, *A History of the Eragny Press* (London: Oak Knoll, 2004); *In Fine Print: William Morris as a Book Designer* (London: London Borough of Waltham Forest, Libraries and Arts Department, 1976); or Roderick Cave, *Fine Printing and Private Presses* (London: British Library, 2001).

16
William Morris, 'How I Became a Socialist', in *Political Writings of William Morris*, ed. A.L. Morton (New York: International Publishers, 1973), p. 241.

times, registering a contempt for

> those articles of folly and luxury ... [that] I will for ever refuse to call wealth: they are not wealth but waste. Wealth is ... what a reasonable man can make out of the gifts of Nature for his reasonable use.[17]

Later, in 1893 and 1894, Morris gave two lectures entitled 'Waste', indicating that the topic had remained a central preoccupation during his years at Kelmscott Press.[18]

Labour and Materials

This illuminates a central tension in Morris's design career and in his vision of the responsible object: how to privilege the durable and the sustainable without privileging those who can afford the durable and sustainable. Many critics have reasonably argued that the Kelmscott Press failed to negotiate this tension: William Peterson's history of Kelmscott, for example, says its books were 'intended to symbolize a protest against the ethos of Victorian industrial capitalism [but] became themselves, in all their opulent splendour, an example of conspicuous consumption'.[19] But Kelmscott's distinctive design was also a means of declaring and foregrounding the artisanal methods and handcrafted materials that were used to produce the books. By presenting such a sharp contrast with other books of the day, they made a critique of mass-produced objects and the kinds of labour and materials that constitute mass production. Kelmscott books ask us to think about the book as a manufactured object, and to think about the kind of labour involved in their production.

17

William Morris, 'Useful Work Versus Useless Toil', in *Political Writings*, p. 91.

18

While sadly no text of these lectures remains, we can see Morris's interest in the idea of waste from the titles of his lectures, which turned to the topics of 'Waste' and 'Makeshift' (a term for cheap goods) in his final years, even as his speaking engagements were decreasing due to poor health. He presented, for example, two lectures in Manchester in 1894: 'Waste' at the Manchester Free Trade Hall, and 'Makeshift' for the Ancoats Brotherhood. Edmund and Ruth Frow, *William Morris in Manchester and Salford* (Salford: Working Class Movement Library, 1996), pp. 22–23.

19

William S. Peterson, *The Kelmscott Press: A History of William Morris's Typographical Adventure* (Oxford: Clarendon, 1991), p. 275.

The last page of each book does this quite specifically, as on the final page of the Kelmscott Chaucer:

> Here ends the Book of the Works of Geoffrey Chaucer, edited by F.S. Ellis; ornamented with pictures designed by Sir Edward Burne-Jones, and engraved on wood by W.H. Hooper. Printed by me William Morris at the Kelmscott Press, Upper Mall, Hammersmith, in the county of Middlesex, finished on the 8th day of May, 1896.

Plenty of other workers were involved in the book's production beyond those recognized on its final page, of course. Typically, the Kelmscott books recognize only Morris and the book's artist or editor; engravers are not always recognized, and compositors and pressmen never are, nor are the men who made the paper and the ink. But if the books do not openly acknowledge every hand that lent itself to their production, they do exemplify, as objects, a mode of production associated with worker-friendly ideals of labour. The press itself, for example, was unionized and paid a good wage. To head its printing operations, Morris brought in Thomas Binning, a staunch trade unionist, and production proceeded in a friendly workshop manner, as John Dreyfus describes:

> industrial relations at the Kelmscott Press were normally very good. Morris enjoyed talking and listening to his compositors, and has been described by an eyewitness as 'taking in every movement of their hands, and every detail of their tools, until he knew as much as they did of spacing, justification and all the rest'. He also spent hours with his pressmen, familiarizing himself with every peculiarity of their doings.[20]

20 John Dreyfus, 'William Morris: Typographer', in *William Morris and the Art of the Book* (New York: Pierpont Morgan Library, 1976), p. 82.

Elizabeth Carolyn Miller

The press was still capitalist—Morris supplied the capital and paid others for their labour, though he also worked beside them—but it pointed the way toward another possible world of production, where the workers and the materials mattered more than profit or scale.

Morris himself spoke openly of the conflict Kelmscott faced between materials and production on the one hand and cost on the other. In 'A Note on ... Founding the Kelmscott Press' he describes how the press used handmade paper, natural inks, and hand labour to make things of beauty that would last and last. Kelmscott's prices were a necessary evil to model a form of production driven by sustainability rather than volume, as Morris said in an 1893 interview:

> I wish—I wish indeed that the cost of the books was less, only that is impossible if the printing and the decoration and the paper and the binding are to be what they should be.[21]

What they should be, for Morris, is not a disposable waste product, like most books of his day, built to sell and not to last. In this sense, Kelmscott was in direct opposition to print's apparently disposable nature. Elizabeth Eisenstein, historian of the printing press, has argued that to some extent print has always been associated with an ideology of disposability:

> printing required the use of paper—a less durable material than parchment or vellum to begin with, and one that has become ever more perishable as the centuries have passed'. When paper reached the point where it might be 'consigned to trash bins or converted into pulp,

21
'"Master Printer Morris": A Visit to the Kelmscott Press', in *The Daily Chronicle* 22 February 1893, rpt. in William Morris, *The Ideal Book: Essays and Lectures on the Arts of the Book*, ed. William S. Peterson (Berkeley: University of California Press, 1982), p. 98.

22

Elizabeth Eisenstein, *The Printing Revolution in Early Modern Europe*, 2nd ed. (Cambridge: Cambridge University Press, 2005), p. 88.

it was 'not apt to prompt thoughts about prolonged preservation'.[22] Yet 'prolonged preservation' was exactly what Morris began to aim at with his Kelmscott Press books.

Superabundance and Obsolescence

In his 1892 essay 'Some Thoughts on the Ornamented Manuscripts of the Middle Ages', Morris bemoaned 'the present age of superabundance of books', and 'the utilitarian production of makeshifts', which 'has swept away the book producer in its current'.[23] Morris has

23

William Morris, 'Some Thoughts on the Ornamented Manuscripts of the Middle Ages', in Morris, *The Ideal Book*, p. 1.

often been accused of elitism, for being a socialist who seemingly prefers books to be rare and artistic rather than cheap and abundant, but notice that it is not the abundance of books that bothers him but the 'superabundance'. His emphasis on 'superabundance' echoes the *Communist Manifesto*'s disgust at the absurd 'epidemic of overproduction' that characterizes capitalist modernity: the waste, glut, and superfluity that run next to poverty and privation.[24] This paradoxical connection between overabundance and want, which Marx and Engels saw as a key feature of capitalism, suggests that deprivation does not result from scarcity but from distribution. For Morris, more cheap books and more cheap goods will not balance the ledger of social equality; an entirely new system is required. This was a central concern of Morris's work. In his novel *A Dream of John Ball*,[25] for example, which was originally serialized in Morris's socialist newspaper and later published in a Kelmscott edition, the narrator travels back in time to the fourteenth century and tries to describe the economic conditions of late-nineteenth-century England. His medieval peasant listener is confused by the horrific idea that 'times of plenty shall in those days

24

Karl Marx and Friedrich Engels, *The Communist Manifesto*, 1848, in Marx, *Selected Writings*, ed. Lawrence H. Simon (Indianapolis: Hackett, 1994), p. 163.

25

E. Burne-Jones, artwork for the first book edition of William Morris's *A Dream of John Ball*, 1888.

Elizabeth Carolyn Miller

A SOCIETY IN WHICH THERE SHOULD BE NEITHER RICH NOR POOR, NEITHER MASTER NOR MASTER'S MAN,

NEITHER IDLE NOR
OVERWORKED,
NEITHER BRAIN-SICK
BRAIN WORKERS NOR
HEART-SICK
HAND WORKERS

be the times of famine'.[26] In Morris's 1891 romance *The Story of the Glittering Plain*, which was also produced in a Kelmscott edition, the titular fantasy land is supposedly a place of superabundance and 'pleasure without cease'—not unlike the department stores that had begun to appear in late-Victorian cities—yet Morris's narrative unmasks it as a corrupt place, a 'land of lies'.[27]

Morris's loathing of mass-produced objects may have begun as a reaction against their ugliness, but in his late work he is more alert to the ethical problems associated with their production as well as their wasteful consumption. He is not alone, of course, in conceptualizing waste as a key component of capitalism: as twentieth-century industrial designer Brooks Stevens famously established by using the term 'planned obsolescence', if a product is not sufficiently transient—in design, function, or performance—people will have no reason to buy another a few years down the road.[28] As a book designer, Morris worked along opposite lines. Many critics have noted the neo-medieval aesthetic of the Kelmscott books, but Morris's goal was actually to 'move out of the historical style, particularly the eclecticism that characterized the Victorian age, into a more ahistorical style'.[29] He drew on older forms in an effort to evoke a kind of temporal neutrality. The types that he designed for Kelmscott, for example, were meant to be 'pure in form', without excessive protuberances.[30] His goal—unmet, perhaps—was to create a durable, timeless style.

Obsolescence in all its forms is, by contrast, key to capitalist models of consumption. Bernard London's 1932 pamphlet *Ending the Depression through Planned Obsolescence* promoted obsolescence as a means of artificially stimulating consumption, thereby stimulating the demand for labour.[31] As London noted, workers appear to *need* overconsumption to protect employment,

26
William Morris, *A Dream of John Ball*, in *Three Works By William Morris*, ed. A.L. Morton (New York: International Publishers, 1986), p. 100.

27
William Morris, *The Story of the Glittering Plain or the Land of Living Men*, facsimile of the 1894 Kelmscott edition (New York: Dover, 1987), pp. 99–100.

28
For more on Brooks Stevens, see Glenn Adamson, *Industrial Strength Design: How Brooks Stevens Shaped Your World* (Boston: MIT Press, 2003).

29
Stansky, *Redesigning the World*, p. 45.

30
Dreyfus, 'William Morris', p. 78.

31
Slade, *Made to Break*, p. 75. Slade notes that this pamphlet was published twenty years before Brooks Stevens claimed to have invented the term 'planned obsolescence'.

but Morris saw this as a waste of labour as well as a waste of material. His lecture 'Art under Plutocracy' challenges the assumption that all labour is necessarily a good regardless of what it produces:

> This doctrine of the sole aim of manufacture (or indeed of life) being the profit of the capitalist and the occupation of the workman, is held, I say, by almost every one; its corollary is, that labour is necessarily unlimited, and that to attempt to limit it is not so much foolish as wicked, whatever misery may be caused to the community by the manufacture and sale of the wares made.[32]

32
William Morris, 'Art under Plutocracy', in *Political Writings of William Morris*, ed. A.L. Morton (New York: International Publishers, 1973), p. 74.

33
Ibid., p. 80.

Morris concluded, in fact, 'the very essence of competitive commerce is waste'.[33] In a better world, workers' livelihood would not depend upon overconsumption, waste, and overwork.

News from Nowhere

34

Kelmscott Manor depicted in the frontispiece to the Kelmscott Press edition of William Morris's *News from Nowhere,* 1893.

Morris depicted such a better world in his 1890 utopian novel *News from Nowhere,*[34] which envisions a future socialist society where nothing is wasted yet nothing is wanted. Of course this is a fantasy, written in a fantasy novel, yet it reminds us that consumer capitalism also depends on a fantasy of waste—an opposite fantasy that de-emphasizes the longevity of objects and the material problem of garbage. Morris's socialist utopia calls attention to this capitalist fantasy by depicting a future society where things do not simply disappear when discarded: objects endure, and people expect them to endure. The future society of Nowhere has overcome environmental pollution and overproduction

Elizabeth Carolyn Miller

by thoroughly internalizing the values of craft, durability, and preservation—central values of the Kelmscott Press. Achieving such a balance requires a resistance to novelty as well as a commitment to making objects that bear conserving. In one illustrative scene, William Guest, a visitor from the nineteenth-century past, goes 'shopping' for a new pipe. Morris counters the inevitable objection to 'communist shopping'—that if all goods are free, people will be wasteful—by depicting the residents of Nowhere as frugal preservationists who expect everything they use to be a durable form of art. When Guest is offered a beautiful pipe from a young shop-girl, he initially demurs, fearing the pipe is too valuable for his own use: 'Dear me ... this is altogether too grand for me... Besides, I shall lose it—I always lose my pipes.' The shop-girl responds, 'What will it matter if you do? Somebody is sure to find it, and he will use it, and you can get another.'[35] In Nowhere, a pipe does not magically disappear: it is picked up by someone else who will dust it off and use it. In a society without private property, where ownership is not a measure of self-worth, used goods and old goods do not lose their appeal. Morris offers a vision of a future where the lines between 'trash' and 'treasure' are blurred as a consequence of communal life.

Morris's utopian pipe is an attack on the neophilia, or love of the new, which is an engrained feature of consumer capitalism. Those critics who fault Morris for drawing on the medieval past in creating his utopian vision, rather than creating an altogether *new* world, are perhaps missing a key point of Morris's design philosophy: innovation for the sake of innovation is a market culture value, and Morris's aesthetic task was to subvert, not uphold, such values. One character in *News from Nowhere* articulates this purpose quite clearly in a description of nineteenth-century capitalism as

35
William Morris, *News from Nowhere* (1890), ed. Stephen Arata (Peterborough: Broadview, 2003), p. 86.

the ceaseless endeavour to expend the least amount of labour on any article made, and yet at the same time to make as many articles as possible. To this 'cheapening of production', as it was called, everything was sacrificed: the happiness of the workman at his work, nay, his most elementary comfort and bare health, his food, his clothes, his dwelling, his leisure, his amusement, his education—his, life, in short—did not weigh a grain of sand in the balance against this dire necessity of 'cheap production' of things, a great part of which were not worth producing at all.[36]

36
Morris, *News from Nowhere*, pp. 138-39.

Such 'cheap production' contrasts sharply with the production practices underlying Kelmscott Press, and *News from Nowhere*, which itself appeared in a Kelmscott edition, demonstrates how such an apparently luxurious enterprise can actually model crucial socialist ideals: durability and sustainability.

Preservation and Persistence

Morris's penchant for durability and preservation is also evident in his active history with the Society for the Protection of Ancient Buildings, familiarly known as the 'Anti-Scrape' Society, which he founded in 1877 and remained involved in until his death in 1896. His work in establishing this society was simultaneous with his increasing involvement in leftist politics, culminating in a conversion to socialism in the early 1880s. The concurrence was not accidental. As E.P. Thompson notes in discussing Morris's rage at the possible destruction of a beautiful, old Berkshire barn: 'It may seem an unlikely road to Communism by way of Great Coxwell

Elizabeth Carolyn Miller

Barn' yet 'Morris's work for the Anti-Scrape contributed as much to bring him on the final stages of his journey as any other influence' because it 'deepened his insight into the destructive philistinism of capitalist society'.[37] Morris's perseverance in preserving old buildings went hand-in-hand with his commitment to common wealth and shared public good over and above individual property. The very idea of the Anti-Scrape Society was infused with a respect for the workers who had produced the buildings in the first place, as well as the materials and labour that made them, and Morris's work for the society also bespeaks his dedication to preservation as a form of historical memory. The responsibility for objects, as this suggests, lies in their production as well as in their use and preservation.

Morris's writing as well as his design calls our attention to material persistence and to the limitations of a capitalist conception of waste as that which readily disappears. Still, a central tension endures in Morris's work regarding the accessibility of sustainable goods, for Morris was not able to democratize durability, and the Kelmscott Press is perhaps the most obvious instance of this since the books have remained extremely expensive into the twenty-first century. Kelmscott allowed Morris to make a point, however, that could not be made by way of cheap print: that waste is a problem of production, that longevity and disposability must be taken into account at the genesis of an object's life, not just the end. In capitalism, waste disposal has traditionally been viewed as the provenance of the consumer rather than the producer, and environmental measures have long emphasized responsible consumption while ignoring responsible production.[38] Today, 'cleaner production' and 'cradle-to-cradle' design are recognized as key environmental measures, but Morris's analysis of waste suggests that this kind of thinking was already

37
E.P. Thompson, *William Morris: Romantic to Revolutionary* (New York: Pantheon, 1955), p. 233.

38
Only in 1989 did the United Nations Environmental Programme launch its 'Cleaner Production' initiative, in an effort to generate 'a preventative approach to environmental management.' United Nations Environmental Programme, Sustainable Consumption and Production Branch, 'Understanding Cleaner Production', www.unep.fr/scp/cp/understanding.

germinating in his nineteenth-century critique of capitalist production. Morris offers a vision of production in
which an object's future life, in all its half-lives, is of more
concern than the scale and speed of its manufacture.
For this reason, the Kelmscott Press articulates a central premise of Morris's socialism in modelling a form
of production grounded in beauty, materials, durability,
and good labour practices, even for that most utilitarian
of arts—bookmaking. It was not enough for Morris to
imbue household objects with the aura of artistic creation, as he did in his work for Morris & Co.; he brought
this aura to the sphere of print, too, to demonstrate that
even an area of production thought to be essentially
indifferent to beauty and craftsmanship could be transformed with a new approach to labour and materials
and with an eye toward future duration.

This contribution was adapted from the author's article 'Sustainable
Socialism: William Morris on Waste', originally published in *The Journal of
Modern Craft* 4, no. 1 (March 2011), pp. 7-25.

Elizabeth Carolyn Miller

A Political Education
The Historical Legacy of the German Bauhaus and the Moscow VKhUTEMAS

Éva Forgács

Material equilibrium of the environment and control of the waste that emerges as a by-product of mass-produced objects is conducive to socially committed design, which is not exclusively aimed at an incessantly accelerated production for the market. Glancing back at the history of modern urban and object planning we can see that many designers took the environment into consideration already at a time when an environmental catastrophe was far from being a widely acknowledged threat to life on Earth.

After the First World War, the history of modern design opened a new chapter in both Germany and Soviet Russia,[1] as new societies were to be built in these countries. They had to be reconstructed from the material poverty of war destruction, and previous under-development, respectively. Germany was declared a Republic on November 9, 1918, and was ruled by the Social Democratic Party—an epochal change after having been an Empire. The Russian Empire, on the other hand, was turned into a Communist state by the revolution of October 25, 1917 (Old style calendar)[2] after the intermezzo of the February 1917 revolution that had already ended the Monarchy.

Material goods were scarce in post-war Germany as well as in post-revolutionary Russia, making systematic production an urgent necessity. Design, as precondition of industrial production, was soon understood in both Germany and Russia as one of the key factors shaping the everyday life of the citizens. Under the new historical conditions the social role and responsibility of the designer was seen in a new light: the use of materials and resources had consequences for the entire economy, and design was instrumental in creating a new lifestyle, implying political consequences as well: affordability and availability of goods would guarantee the satisfaction and optimism of the population. There

1
The name of the country 'Soviet Union' was adapted in December 1922.

2
The Gregorian Calendar (New Style) was introduced in Russia on February 14, 1918. According to this, the Revolution's date is November 7.

Éva Forgács

was, indeed, a sense of a new beginning both in Germany and Russia: the construction of a new world awakened the designers to their new potential and task.

The vital economic and political importance of design was recognized in Germany already at the turn of the twentieth century when the rapid industrialization forced huge numbers of people to migrate to the cities to find jobs. This mass relocation made it urgent for the industrialists, architects and artists to find ways to provide the new urban residents with the basics, and make decisions about either switching to mass production mode or sticking to quality-centred manufacturing. The Deutscher Werkbund was organized in 1907[3] as a platform for the opposing views in these issues. The conflict between supporters of mass production and those of artistic autonomy was not resolved in the years leading up to the start of the Great War in 1914, but it highlighted the increased economic and aesthetic weight of industrial design already in the pre-war period.

The Bauhaus: Economy on Small and Large Scale

In the wake of the War, when, in the midst of political chaos and poverty, progressive artists re-organized the cultural landscape of Germany, the designer's ethical and social commitment was recognized anew. Architect Walter Gropius opened the Bauhaus school with a Manifesto depicting a utopian vision of collective creative work, which respectfully dismissed grand art as a gift that, due to 'grace of heaven', may, or may not emerge from craftsmanship, and instead proposed object making as the foundation of all creative work.[4]

Gropius was convinced that the fundamental conflict between industrial design and artistic autonomy could not be overcome immediately. He saw a solution

3
Organizers and leading figures were, among others, Peter Behrens, Theodor Fischer, Hermann Muthesius, Bruno Paul, Richard Riemerschmid, Henry van de Velde, Walter Gropius.

4
Walter Gropius, *Manifesto*. Independent leaflet, circulated in 1919 prior to the opening of the Bauhaus in Weimar.

Lyonel Feininger, The Cathedral of Socialism, cover of the Bauhaus Manifesto by Walter Gropius, 1919.

in a longer process that could be achieved throughout education, the training of a new generation of visual experts who would be equally competent in both fields. However, the post-war conditions did not allow him to introduce design education in the Bauhaus: he had to be content with starting the school's programme with the crafts, which did not require an industrial background. Budgeted by the Social Democrat-run Parliament of Thüringen, the Bauhaus opened in Weimar on April 11, 1919, as a merger of the former Grand Ducal School of Arts and Crafts, and the Grand Ducal Saxon Art Academy. The limited funds the school had at its disposal amidst the shortages of the country made it necessary to find economical solutions in every field of their activities. This implied, even if not out of environmental awareness, reducing the institute's carbon footprint to a minimum. For one thing, coal was in short supply, but ethical considerations were also important. The combination of a low budget and social responsibility soon led to the guiding principle of what we call sustainability today. Renewal of architecture was on Gropius's and his colleague Bruno Taut's minds already in 1918, when Taut wrote a new 'Architecture Programme', reflecting their shared ideas envisioning buildings 'not in the city but on open land', because 'the future lies in the newly developed land which will nourish itself'.[5] The idea was to replace metropolitan areas with new types of settlements proposed by a collaborative council of architects and landscape designers. As part of anticipating such a project, the Bauhaus started its own vegetable garden on its own plot of land to provide food for its kitchen, under the duress of the inflationary times in 1923.[6]

Saving on costs was consistent with designing affordable goods, and remained a basic requirement in the Bauhaus even after Gropius had left the school in 1928.

5
Bruno Taut, 'Architektur-Programm' (December 1918), in *Programme und Manifeste zur Architektur des 20. Jahrhunderts*, ed. Ulrich Conrads (Berlin: Birkhäuser, 1964), p. 38.

6
Stenographic minutes of the session of the Parliament of Thüringen, 1923, reprinted in Karl-Heinz Hüter, *Das Bauhaus in Weimar* (Berlin: Akademie-Verlag, 1976), p. 244. See also Magdalene Droste, *Bauhaus* (Cologne: Taschen, 2006), p. 42.

Éva Forgács

Awareness of full use of material and avoiding losses were of great importance for example in Josef Albers's Preliminary Course.[7] He stressed the supreme importance of eliminating waste, calling attention to the negative shapes of the materials that were cut out, but had to be made useful as well. One of the students, Hans Beckmann, writes in his memoir:

> Josef Albers entered the classroom with a bundle of newspapers under his arm. 'Ladies and gentlemen,' he said, 'we are poor and not rich. We cannot afford to waste materials or time. Every piece of work has a starting material, and therefore we must examine the nature of this material. ... I would like you to take these newspapers in hand and make something more out of them than what they are at present. ... If you can do so without any accessories, such as cutters, scissors or glue, all the better.[8]

When evaluating the students' works Albers underlined that a piece of newspaper lying on the table has only one visually active side, while the same newspaper, when turned upright, reveals both of its sides, doubling its visual activity without any expense of work or energy. Beckmann added that after some time the students started to see material in such a way and were considering aspects of economy when working.[9] They tried to spare both material and work. 'No unused residuals must be left at the making of any form' Albers advised, 'or the calculation is not correct. ... Material economy implies discipline, and purity and precision are the greatest discipline factors.'[10] Economical use of material, historian Rainer Wick notes, leads to clean shapes and lightness, both highly accepted values in the Bauhaus, demonstrated, for example, by Marcel Breuer's tubular chair series.[11]

7
Josef Albers was teaching the Preliminary Course along with László Moholy-Nagy from 1923. After Moholy-Nagy left the Bauhaus in 1928, Albers was the leading teacher of the Preliminary Course.

Josef Albers's Bauhaus preliminary class, photo by Umbo (Otto Umbehr) 1928. © The Josef and Anni Albers Foundation.

8
Rainer Wick, *Bauhaus Pädagogik* (Cologne: DuMont Buchverlag, 1982), pp. 165-67.

9
Ibid., p. 167.

10
Ibid.

11
Ibid.

Woman (Lis Beyer or Ilse Gropius) sitting in B3 club chair by Marcel Breuer, wearing a mask by Oskar Schlemmer and dress fabric by Herbert Beyer, photo by Erich Consemüller, c. 1926.

The juxtaposition of positive and negative forms and an emphasis on their equality are demonstrated in many student works as well as in Gropius's Bauhaus building in Dessau where the convex (positive, protruding) forms generate concave (negative, inwardly curving) spaces, both of which are quintessential aesthetic as well as practical. According to Albers, studies of the equal functionality of positive forms and the negative spaces they create, transcend aesthetics: besides eliminating waste, 'this is a metaphor of the understanding of democracy that negates the difference between dominating and dominated, ruler and the ruled', and thus it is an indirect political education.[12]

12
Quoted and commented by Wick, *Bauhaus Pädagogik*, p. 169.

VKhUTEMAS, the Educational Model of the Russian Revolution

The Bauhaus's Russian counterpart, the VKhUTEMAS[13] also came into being via the merger of an academy of fine arts and a school of applied arts—SVOMAS I,[14] successor of the former Moscow Stroganoff School of Applied Arts, and SVOMAS II, created from the former Moscow Academy of Painting. VKhUTEMAS was established in 1920 by a decree of the People's Commissariat with the purpose of educating artist-designers as well as instructors and leaders in the field of professional technical education. The decree had the signatures of V.I. Lenin, President of the People's Commissariat, and of the leader of the Secretariat thereof, V. Bonch-Bruyevich.

The VKhUTEMAS, which operated in Moscow from 1920 to 1930, shared many concepts with the Bauhaus both in far-sighted social utopias and down-to-earth responses to the actual material needs of society. In 1928 it was re-named VKhUTEIN, Higher Artistic and

13
Vysshie khudozhestvenno-tekhnicheskie masterskie: Higher Artistic and Technical Studios.

14
Svobodnie Masterskie: Free Workshops.

Éva Forgács

THE MOST IMPORTANT THING IS TO

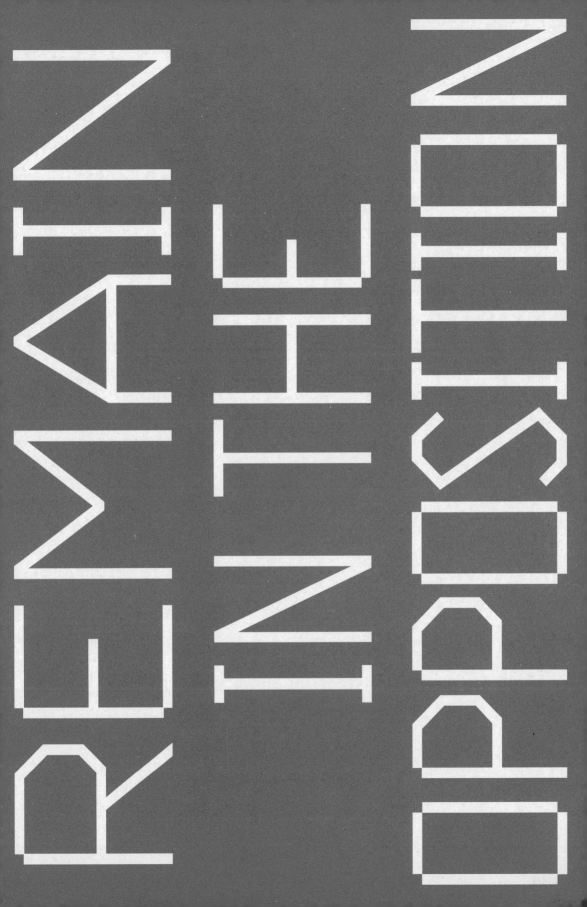

Technical Institution, becoming more institutionalized, similar to the Bauhaus' 1926 switch from calling the faculty teachers 'master' to granting them the title of 'professor'.

The faculty of the VKhUTEMAS included leading representatives of various movements of the Russian avant-gardes, such as Constructivism, represented by painter and sculptor Alexander Rodchenko and his wife, textile designer Varvara Stepanova. The constructivist group's fundamental concepts were anti-aesthetic and proposed three-dimensional, real-material constructions in real space, with a 'utilitarian imperative'.[15] Pre-dating Josef Albers's teachings and independently from him, they theorized the necessity to create economical constructions as an ethical duty of the designer. Constructivism was launched in March 1921 in another institution, the Moscow INKhUK[16] by, among others, Rodchenko and Stepanova. Constructivism entailed the minimum of material and work expenditure for maximum results; and the creation of constructions, which do not include any 'excess materials and excess elements'.[17] If any part of the construction could be removed without destroying the entire piece, the work did not qualify as a construction and was not acceptable.

Multimedia artist Vladimir Tatlin, who was on the faculty of the VKhUTEMAS during the years 1927–1931, pursued concepts very similar to those of Josef Albers. His 'functional worker's outfit' was designed with 'the cut-out patterns included',[18] attempting to entirely avoid waste of material. Tatlin also built a stove 'in the hard days of 1918–1919 to consume the minimum of fuel while giving maximum heat'.[19] Among the economical projects of the school were such objects as the students of the Metal Faculty ('Metfak') presented in 1923, in three groups:

15
Christina Lodder, *Russian Constructivism* (London and New Haven: Yale University Press, 1983), p. 83.

16
Institut Khudozhestvennoi Kul'tury: Institute of Artistic Culture.

17
Varvara Stepanova at the January 28, 1921 session of the Constructivists, quoted by Lodder, *Russian Constructivism*, p. 88.

18

Tatlin's New Way of Life, newspaper article with Tatlin showing his functional worker's outfit, coat, and stove, 1924.

19
For more details see Camilla Gray: *The Russian Experiment in Art 1863–1922* (London: Thames & Hudson, 1962), p. 236, and Lodder, *Russian Constructivism*, p. 155.

1: Dissectible objects that could be folded after use (Kiosks that could be assembled and disassembled after use; folding beds); 2: Multi-functional objects (sofa bed, drawing table that turns into bed, etc.); and, 3: Objects that can be disassembled when moving them (movable bookshelves, etc.).[20]

For example, Rodchenko's Workers' Club,[21] exhibited at the Exposition Internationale des Arts Décoratifs et Industriels Modernes in Paris in 1925, was not only economical in its use of space and material, but the items had to be collapsible, too, for easy removal and storage.[22] Assembling and disassembling objects as well as designing multi-functional ones was a widespread practice in modern design. What distinguished such designs at the Bauhaus[23] and the VKhUTEMAS[24] from similar, merely practical experiments in other countries was the ethical overtone that was driving designers to serve society, which Albers interpreted as the concept of democracy. In Russia, in the midst of scarcity of material and technologies, to make the most out of the least was a political act in the service of the people and the new state.

Varvara Stepanova's activity at the VKhUTEMAS, where she was appointed professor at the Textile Department in 1923, is another example of radically new and, *avant la lettre*, sustainable textile design. On the one hand, she wanted to reform fabric production by creating newly structured, layered textiles for 'organic' rather than painted patterns; on the other hand, she designed geometrically stylized clothes[25] that would not only look modern, but would also eliminate waste of material generated by the ragged outlines of the cut-out pattern. She pioneered the concept that 't he cut of a garment and the design of the fabric should be

20
Alina Abramova, 'Vchute-mas—Vchutein (1918–1930)', *Rassegna sovietica* 18, no. 4 (1968), pp. 128–42.

21

Interior of Rodchenko's Workers Club shown at the Soviet pavilion, Exposition Internationale des Arts Décoratifs et Industriels Modernes, 1925.

22
Lodder, *Russian Constructivism*, p. 156.

23
At the Bauhaus, student Alma Buscher designed multi-functional furniture for children for the 1923 Bauhaus exhibition's experimental house, the Haus am Horn: coloured, larger and smaller hollow cubes, to be used as tables and chairs, or elements of construction to play with, or, pushed together, as a surface to sit or sleep on.

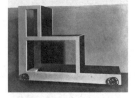

Alma Buscher, ladder chair for children's room, 1923. © 2015 Lucia Moholy Estate.

24
See, for example, Galaktionov's, Zemlyanitsyn's or Sobolev's multi-functional furniture designed 1927–1929 in El Lissitzky's workshop, that open up to become sleepers, storage units, or desks.

Éva Forgács

worked out simultaneously',[26] and that the textile industry 'jettison its present excessive variety, and help it standardize and improve',[27] for a new, socialist quality of life.

Then again, material limitations inspired architects and designers to think big about a sustainable future. For example, one the students of VKhUTEMAS' Department of Architecture, Georgii Krutikov (1899–1958), considered architectural planning as the planning of the future of humankind. He observed that transportation had significantly developed over the centuries, and that the various vehicles that mankind invented 'could be regarded as mobile architecture'.[28] So, unlike Gropius and Taut, he considered saving the land entirely, and detaching architecture from the ground as a future possibility. As his monographer put it,

> For Krutikov, land was vital to human beings, above all, because it enabled them to create favourable conditions for people on Earth. Was it absolutely necessary, therefore, to cover it with buildings? The dispersal of human settlements throughout the world limited man's potential to use land effectively in the interests of society as a whole.[29]

In our current terms it is adequate to say that Krutikov considered the sustainability of life on Earth and addressed this issue head-on. He did not go into such details as the circulation of material, waste production and recycling, but he anticipated that a growing populaion would exhaust the natural resources. Therefore, in his diploma work Krutikov displayed statistical information concerning the world's population growth, the percentage of land covered by water, ice, deserts, et cetera. He argued that the amount of the world's land

25

Varvara Stepanova, sports clothes projects in *LEF* magazine, 1923.

26
Alexander Lavrentiev, *Varvara Stepanova: The Complete Work* (Cambridge: The MIT Press, 1988), p. 79.

27
Ibid., p. 81.

28
Selim Khan-Magomedov, *Georgii Krutikov: The Flying City and Beyond*, trans. Christina Lodder (Barcelona: Tenov Books, 2015), p. 12.

Georgii Krutikov, The Flying City, 1928.

29
Ibid., p. 12.

mass that was suitable for humanity's use was limited, and the rapid territorial expansion of the world's population would produce considerable difficulties in the future. '... Krutikov placed particular emphasis on the limited space in contemporary large cities ... and then showed preparatory sketches, which depicted a city in the sky.'[30]

Krutikov's ideas were received by most of his professors and fellow students as fantastic, utopian, and not suitable for practical purposes, while he continued to study moving forms, their possible trajectories and dynamics.[31]

Parallels That Do Not Meet

In spite of seeking intersections—meeting points and even cooperation[32]—their similar concepts notwithstanding, the Bauhaus and the VKhUTEMAS operated in different political and historical spaces and their respective views on service to society were, in many ways, directly opposite. For example, the Bauhaus started out as an avant-garde centre in opposition to mainstream culture, but became a fashionable school of architecture and design with successful products by the end of the 1920s. By way of contrast, the VKhUTEMAS was founded as a fully state-supported school only to have its artists, activities and products marginalized by the end of the 1920s. These opposing trajectories indicate the different roles that design played in Germany and Soviet Russia, the Bauhaus's rationalist design concepts tending to serve the economy, whereas the VKhUTEMAS' design concepts were subordinated to political ideology.

Their histories also diverged. The Bauhaus came into existence in a defeated country that expected a

30
Ibid., pp. 12–13.

31
Leaving the land mass is also a contemporary concept. For example, Belgian ecological architect Vincent Callebaut has developed plans for a city of futuristic ocean buildings made from 3D-printed plastic waste, which extend into the ocean's water and appear to float on the surface.

32
For details about attempts to establish contacts, see Annemarie Jaeggi, 'Relations between the Bauhaus and the Russian Avant-garde as Documented in the Collection of the Bauhaus Archive Berlin', in *Moscow—Berlin: Interchanges and Heritage of the 20th Century*, pp. 154–57, www.icomos. org/risk/2007/pdf/Soviet_Heritage_34_V-4_ Jaeggi.pdf.

revolution, a country whose hopes were not yet quite dashed in 1919. The school faced increasingly violent opposition and hostility in its immediate environment, forcing it to be on the defensive during most of its entire history. Rationalism and economizing in production were meant to serve the community, but they did not square with German traditionalism. As opposed to the Bauhaus' position, the VKhUTEMAS was the brainchild of a victorious revolution; the avant-garde elevated to the status of official art, consecrated by the signatures of the state's leaders, regardless of its popular recognition or lack thereof.

The Bauhaus had to struggle to have its progressive designs accepted. In the process, it gave up bits and pieces of its independence in the hope of retaining the greater part of the same. In contrast, the VKhUTEMAS was basically—if not in every detail—identified with the new, revolutionary state: it was directed by artists who were themselves the developers and directors of the state's art policies. For example, as Christina Lodder, one of the best art historians about the era writes, 'to Rodchenko construction represented the culmination of centuries of artistic development. It was part of the same process that had previously produced communist Russia. It was its artistic equivalent.'[33] VKhUTEMAS was the art school, where the state intended to train its own upcoming generation of artists, in the spirit of its own ideology. At the outset there was hardly any distance, let alone opposition, between the state and the art school. The Bauhaus, by contrast, remained in the position of art as opposition and resistance. Gropius had even defined this as a programme: 'The most important thing is to remain in the opposition. This way one stays fresh.'[34] The Bauhaus kept on attempting to convince the conservative majority of Germany of the superior quality of its minimalist, economical, mod-

33
Lodder, *Russian Constructivism*, p. 88.

34
Walter Gropius, letter to Adolph Behne, September 16, 1919, in Hüter, *Das Bauhaus in Weimar*, p. 213.

ernist designs, eventually with some success. In total contrast to this, the VKhUTEMAS was in a position of power, while the large majority that did not understand or did not favour their new formal language and considered the new works anarchic and impenetrable, was temporarily muzzled.[35]

In Germany in the mid-1920s, the economic consolidation, accompanied by a temporary political respite, also dulled the edge of the opposition, transferring resistance more and more from the field of politics to the professional issues of art and design. In 1923–24 there was a glimmer of hope that the Bauhaus might achieve both intellectual and practical—that is, financial—autonomy, and reach a rational relationship with society by serving its needs according to its non-ideological, economical principles and design practices. The situation of Soviet artists and of VKhUTEMAS was radically different, since, as soldiers of the revolution, they all relied on state support. This support was based on political trustworthiness, and, as history amply demonstrates, ceased with that trust. Therefore the rationalism and economical aspects of design were subordinated to political decisions.

In stark contrast to a market economy, political decrees regulated the Soviet Union's production processes. As Lodder relates,

> A nationwide 'Regime of Economy' was launched by the Party Central Committee in June 1926, and was followed in March of the following year by another decree launching a campaign for the 'Rationalization of Production' on all fronts ... stressing the impersonal aspects of design and minimizing the role of subjective criteria.[36]

35
See, for example, Ilya Ehrenburg, *Emberek, évek, életem* [People, years and life], trans. Ános Elbert (Budapest: Gondolat, 1963), Part II, p. 271: 'The futurists thought that people's tastes could be changed as rapidly as the economic structure of society. In *Iskusstvo kommuny* one would read, "We indeed claim, and would hardly resist the opportunity to use, government power for the realization of our art". Etc.'

36
Lodder, *Russian Constructivism*, p. 137.

Éva Forgács

The End of Free Education of Art and Design

The Bauhaus was expelled from Dessau in 1932 when the Nazi Party won the regional elections in Saxen-Anhalt, and, after a very successful semester as Mies van der Rohe's private school in Berlin, dissolved itself after the Nazi takeover. Mies van der Rohe attempted to negotiate with the new Minister of Culture, but he was dictated certain conditions, such as firing some of the faculty members in order to stay in business. The faculty of the Bauhaus, under this pressure, then collectively issued a document about terminating the Bauhaus because of 'financial difficulties'.

The VKhUTEMAS ceased to exist as an independent school in 1930, as its Architectural Faculty was incorporated in the Higher Engineering and Architectural Institute, later called the Moscow Architectural Institute. This happened at a time when the Soviet avant-garde fell increasingly out of favour, and Stalin's hard-line politics were consolidating. In the field of culture this process led to the declaration of Socialist Realism as the only acceptable and 'official' style in literature and the visual arts at the First Congress of Soviet Writers in 1934.

As the histories of both the Bauhaus and the VKhUTEMAS indicate, environmentally responsible design was in the books, even if under different headings. Economizing with resources for either purely economic, or both political and economic purposes was required in both cases, driven by ethical considerations to serve a larger purpose than the direct use of the designed object. As the plight of the two schools demonstrates, the political significance of putting design in the service of the public good could last only under at least relatively free political conditions.

Margarete Schütte-Lihotzky
A Career in the Design Politics of the Everyday

Susan R. Henderson

> ... I was part of a group that stood up for certain principles and architectural ideas, and fought for them uncompromisingly.[1]
> – *Margarete Schütte-Lihotzky*

1
Quoted in Burkhardt Rukschcio and Roland Schachel, *Adolf Loos: Leben und Werk* (Vienna: Residenz, 1982), p. 575.

Margarete Schütte-Lihotzky (1897–2000) is widely known as the designer of the Frankfurt Kitchen, but it was in the last decade of her life, and following her death at the age of 103, that she has become a figure of historical stature. As a designer certainly, but also as a political activist, reformer and feminist, a woman who lived a life of courage and determination and unflagging political commitment. From a contemporary vantage point, her life and work assume a fresh resonance in a time of heightened political and social concerns.

Lihotzky's professional struggles as a woman are not difficult to imagine. She was most often the only woman in her professional milieu—the only woman in her class at the Vienna Academy; the only woman architect in Vienna's housing office in 1921—where she worked under Adolf Loos and Oscar Strand—the only woman on Ernst May's design team in the 'New Frankfurt' initiative from 1926 to 1930, and the only woman named a member of the Ernst May Brigade when it travelled to Moscow from 1930 to 1937. And while in these early decades her milieu was politically sympathetic to her leftist, indeed, communist agenda, following the end of the Second World War, she found herself once again ostracized for her political stance as well as her gender.

Throughout her life Lihotzky viewed her architectural practice as fundamental to her political agenda. So aside from being an exemplar of political activism, what design lessons might be gleaned from Lihotzky's career with regard to the sustainability project? Cer-

Susan R. Henderson

tainly her dedication to the everyday is a starting point; and there is a corollary project in public education. Her areas of design expertise can be divided into a few distinct categories. The best known is her work the Frankfurt Kitchen (1927),[2] a distilled version of prior research and a line of Frankfurt kitchens she designed to suit different dwelling types. She began thinking about the modern kitchen when working in Vienna. In 1922, she penned her first article on the kitchen, commissioned by Ernst May, then in Breslau. In it, she declared that new designs would be based on 'scientific principles' and the ideal of rational housekeeping.[3] The primary goal of kitchen design in the 1920s was to save labour, but the basis of these savings was the Taylorized workspace, one in which the space was small and movements 'scientifically calculated' to result in the fewest number of movements of a single worker to complete a particular task.

Along with these spatial strategies, she applied technical ones. Here one sees the introduction of innovative building materials—paramount is Lihotzky's interesting all-concrete kitchen of 1923—and new technologies, in Frankfurt especially electrical appliances.[4] Electricity did enable a remarkable array of labour-saving equipment in the kitchen. The Frankfurt kitchen came with an electric or gas stove, a water heater, a slow-cooker, electric light, and a built-in ironing board, rarities in even middle-class homes in 1927. Now there was no more need to fetch fuel—one of the most laborious of tasks and a dirty one; no need to nurse a fire or heat water on the stove, no need to tend gas light fixtures, and indoor air quality improved considerably. Lihotzky was adamant that such 'luxuries' were affordable in public housing—provided that the economies in space, material, and labour costs were realized—and that the improvements in daily life they afforded should

2

Margarete Schütte-Lihotzky, Frankfurt Kitchen, 1927.

3
Grete Lihotzki [sic], 'Einige über die Einrichtung österreichischer Häuser unter besonderer Berücksichtigung der Siedlungsbauten', *Schlesisches Heim* no. 8, August 1921, pp. 217–22.

4
Sophie Hochhäusl, 'From Vienna to Frankfurt inside Core-House Type 7: A History of Scarcity through the Modern Kitchen', *Architectural Histories* no. 1 (November 2013), pp. 1–19.

not be confined to the wealthier classes. Lihotzky recorded what a battle it was to argue the cost of the Frankfurt Kitchen for the working class in the city council hall, where opponents threatened to curtail funding for such 'extravagances', but it was just one of many such battles she faced during her career in her dedication to the egalitarian distribution of resources.

With its inter-locking parts, its modularity and technical fittings, the Frankfurt kitchen is a prime example of total design. Continuous counter space encircled the housewife; at the short end of the room, the cutting board had its own small waste bin, was directly lit by a window, and provided a swivel stool. To the left was the garbage chute. Dishes were emptied, washed, and stored in one continuous motion, from the waste bin to the sink to the wooden plate holder above or the dish drainer on the right. A row of hooks put an array of special tools to hand; to the side eighteen labelled metal drawers stored flours and other dry goods.

From today's vantage point there are two cautionary lessons issuing from the then common strategies of spatial efficiency and technology as solutions to human environments. First, modelling the kitchen on working kitchens in railway trains and factory workstations, as Lihotzky did, consolidated space, but also brought unforeseen social and labour costs with them. In the small cube of space defined by the Frankfurt Kitchen, the housewife was literally on her own, and, unwittingly perhaps, the workstation idea helped redefine the married woman as a suburban stay-at-home housekeeper, while ignoring the growth in the number of working wives and mothers. In the end, the combination of spatial efficiency and technology did not reduce women's work load, as her isolation put increased burdens squarely on her shoulders, rather than on those of a shared household economy of labour as experienced,

Susan R. Henderson

THE IMPROVEMENTS IN DAILY LIFE SHOULD NOT

BE CONFINED TO THE WEALTHIER CLASSES

for example, in extended family networks and farm life. Secondly, the miracle of electricity posed its own and environmental burdens, and was not the unmixed blessing in the larger social sense that it was envisioned to be.

Lihotzky produced kitchen-related designs throughout her career. In Frankfurt, the USSR, and Ankara, she produced teaching kitchens[5] that prepared girls to assume the role of the modern housewife. Such classrooms included miniature modern kitchens set in a 'laboratory' atmosphere that reflected the ideal of the serious endeavours of the professional housewife setting about the science of 'Home Economics'.

Aside from meal preparation, the second onerous task of housekeeping was laundry, and Lihotzky designed electric laundry facilities[6] for two of the great Frankfurt housing settlements. These facilities considerably eased the physical labour involved in hand washing, water gathering, boiling clothes, and all the rest. Lihotzky calculated that the electric laundry reduced a typical laundry day from fifteen to five hours. In addition, it removed the washing from the cooking area, and wet clothes and linens hanging indoors in inclement weather. Inside Lihotzky's laundry in the settlement of Praunheim were peripheral cubicles, surrounded by textured glass partitions each equipped with a soaking tub, a sink, and a utility table. Along the centre aisle stood eight, large lateral-tumbling washing machines, four centrifuges, and two dehumidifiers, and tall stands each topped by a shallow dish. In a separate room dedicated to drying and ironing, equipped with drying lockers and mangles, rows of laundry lines hung from the exposed beams on the roof. The laundries were a grand success.

Another endeavour that occupied much of Lihotzky's career was the creation of tightly-configured

5

Margarete Schütte-Lihotzky, Frankfurt Home Economics classroom, 1927.

6

Margarete Schütte-Lihotzky, electric laundry, c. 1928.

dwellings with a puzzle-box array of cabinetry and lightweight, mobile, and gender-neutral furniture. Of particular interest are her projects for women. One of the first is an elegant bedsit room designed for a Ms. C. Neubacher in 1925, and now on display in the Museum of Applied Arts (Museum für angewandte Kunst) in Vienna. Again, Lihotzky based the design on a train compartment. The seamless cabinetry that comprises the walls is without embellishment and in a varnished wood, reflecting Adolf Loos's influence. The principle of sparing and economic use of materials, quality detailing, and rationalized space are all here, and sum up several of the primary principles of Lihotzky's design method. Meanwhile, she was already applying the same strategy to the minimal dwelling, exemplifying the same solution in a more humble and socially reforming context. While she pursued her assigned tasks in the minimal dwelling in Vienna and Frankfurt, Lihotzky also undertook proposals for dwellings for single women. As a result of the war, there was a massive population of 'permanently' single women in Europe, and then, too, a growing population of women seeking independence. This raised interest in this new housing type, but it also presented the dual problem of minimum means and social consequence. A model unit for exhibition of 1927–1928, while more modest in materials and comprising an entire dwelling, not merely a retreat, nevertheless shared many of its features. In a space approximately three-meters square, niches side to side accommodated a bed on one side and a kitchenette and washroom on the other. The entry wall comprised built-in storage, with a window wall and balcony facing out on the other side.[7]

Lihotzky's interest in built-in furnishing extended back to her 1917 design for a fold-out dressing table, and extended to projects such as her 1926 competi-

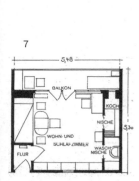

Margarete Schütte-Lihotzky, floor plan of apartment for the single woman, 1927–1928.

Susan R. Henderson

tion entry for a train sleeping compartment. In more complex projects such as the single woman's dwelling of 1927–1928, she plotted movement as a series of hypothetical, linked actions that she translated into arrangements and furnishings that facilitated different uses during the day. Thus the sleeping niche doubled as a seating alcove. Its wood panelling served both as the head- and footboard of a bed, and the backrest of a sofa. A pad fitted with a loose cover substituted for a mattress and spring. Brooms were stored in a cove underneath. She provided an airing cupboard for the bedding, and next to the daybed was a small cupboard that also served as an armrest. When folded out it made a work surface and revealed a divided compartment for needles, thread, and silk, with a drawer to hold mending underneath. A table fronting the daybed folded out for entertaining, as did the tea table.[8]

This comprehensive approach was on view in her full-scale mock-up for the single woman's dwelling of 1927–1928. Lihotzky modelled this life style rather on her own, with the result that it contained little of the womanly features associated with 'proper' women's domains. On exhibit, her one-room apartment represented a largely gender-neutral imagery, and a new kind of freedom for the single woman. Independence, privacy, and a certain leisure were expressed in its simple elements: the balcony,[9] which lay beyond a long, windowed wall, hinted at leisurely afternoons in the company of a book. The fold-down book table performed a kind of coda as did the well-lighted desk.

If these pieces expressed women's liberation from drudgery after a hard day's work, the very small space necessitated by the extravagance of dedicated housing for women in itself dictated the unit would be tightly configured to serve its everyday purposes. Like the Frankfurt Kitchen, it was modelled on the tight spaces

8

Margarete Schütte-Lihotzky, multi-functional furniture in single woman's apartment, 1927–1928.

9

Margarete Schütte-Lihotzky, balcony of apartment designed for the single woman, 1927–1928.

of transportable environments—the train car was an ever-present model—and indeed Lihotzky had produced her own design for a sleeper car in 1926. Like the private train compartment, her single woman's apartment demonstrated that every forethought had been given to the necessities. The kitchen niche and washroom were small and modest. A long wall of built-in cupboards had five compartments, variously assigned to clothes, shoes (an aired cupboard), dishes, food, linens, books, and a pass-through for deliveries.[10] All the furnishings were lacquered (in a rich blue) for easy cleaning; the carpets, covers, and curtains were washable. Lihotzky estimated that with rationalized production, the rent, utilities, and cleaning service would amount to an affordable fifty marks per month.

Another aspect considered in the design of new model furniture was the incipient nomadism of the time. Throughout the upheavals of the interwar period, moving house had become an accepted part of modern life. Said Lihotzky, 'people are mobile and frequently uprooted, so we provide built-ins'.[11] The new furniture made moving simpler, and exchanged, hopefully, the anguish of upheaval for excitement and anticipation, and the comfort of stability for portability. Lightweight generic furnishings also enabled transformability, an idea demonstrated in Paul Wolff's film *Die Frankfurter Kleinstwohnung* (The Frankfurt Minimal Dwelling) (1927). The film, which was staged in a version of Lihotzky's single woman's apartment, followed a 'typical' family of three through the course of a day, as the housewife rearranged the furniture for each occasion. The small square table next to the chesterfield was there for having breakfast in the morning. After the husband departed for work, she stowed it away, and drew out a leafed dining table as a friend arrived for tea. When the husband came home that evening, the

10

Margarete Schütte-Lihotzky, built-in furniture in single woman's apartment, 1927–1928.

11
Margarete Schütte-Lihotzky interviewed in 'Die Frankfurter Küche war ein Umsturz in den Eigentumsverhältnissen', *Frankfurter Stadt-Rundschau* 23 January 1997.

Susan R. Henderson

whole group retired to the terrace where the small table reappeared, and the child was entertained with a set of modern blocks. Similarly, a few components could transform the small space of a single woman's dwelling of 1927 throughout the day.

On the other hand, the super-specificity of her built-in furniture was so specialized to facilitate, but also to limit, the use of space. Lihotzky's 1930 modular furniture line included both kinds of furniture. Moveable furniture 'offered the advantages of spatial adaptability, changeability, and portability', while storage defined and limited the necessities of modern life for the householder. The series included 103 distinct pieces, including six daybeds, seventeen freestanding table types, and ten shelving types. The rest was entirely devoted to highly specific storage pieces. There were seventy closet pieces in which Lihotzky articulated the minutiae of daily habits with tidy components that folded out, and away, nested, and concealed. She differentiated cupboards for clothing, dirty laundry, and airing, sideboards, and sewing cabinets—each had special dividers for cutlery or small items—broom and utility-closets, and writing desks. Accessories included patented clothes hooks, tie holders, screens, and broom holders. It was a remarkable statement about the need for compactness in modern living—for economy's sake, but also for a kind of ascetic piece of mind. It was also conceived as a kind of do-it-yourself custom design. As purchasers moved from one dwelling to another, they could assemble combinations to suit their dwelling, without help of a carpenter. They created 'built-in' furniture by bolting the pieces together, levelling them with setscrews to make the necessary adjustments to the layout. At the same time, the simplicity and organizing principles of the pieces, their small scale, and transformability conserved resources and space, and the life reform issues, such as lessening household chores were firmly embedded in their design.

As the film intended to do, and as the home economics classroom did for the kitchen, Lihotzky envisioned the need for public education in these new life habits, based not on the growing fashionableness of 'the modern' among the upper classes but on the functional advantages of modern equipping in the everyday dwelling. In 1926, she proposed setting up a research and public information office—a kind of advice centre for the household—in the Handwerkerhaus (Craftsman Center) in Frankfurt. She proposed to both produce studies on labour-saving kitchens and built-in furniture, and to advise the public on their advantages and usage. The centre would test new materials and equipment, and design new models and their mechanical interface. She envisioned the production of prospectuses and photos, and publishing 'in all kinds of newspapers and magazines' and the creation of slide presentations— arranged as a series of good and bad examples. The office would further engage housewives' clubs with talks, demonstrations and exhibits, send articles to major city newspapers, and contact influential people and architects.

Lihotzky's work in the area of diminutive house holding produced another effort in the design of garden cabins. She designed her first in Vienna in the early 1920s, then was assigned to design standardized garden cabins for the Frankfurt allotments. Between the years 1927–1930 they were built in the hundreds. Each New Frankfurt apartment dweller was allocated an allotment patch in one of the well-ordered garden colonies near their settlement. Each garden was laid out by the city in a rationalized manner that was likened to that of the kitchen, and each had its own tidy cube

Susan R. Henderson

of a cabin.[12] In the previous decade, ramshackle garden colonies had sprung up on city lands both as a wildcat effort for families to supply themselves with food during the war, and then, more desperately, as ad-hoc housing. In the minds of many the garden cabin, as an ideal, conjured up an idealized, back-to-the-land retreat where one could while away summer afternoons. The Frankfurt Housing Authority imposed uniformity and discipline on the existing 'chaos' of the colonies, while fostering both its idealistic and reform associations. Likewise, Lihotzky's cabin had an efficient organization and was equipped with built-in storage, seating, sleeping benches, and a heating and cooking stove. At the same time, she allowed for its transformation from a storage and utility shed, by means of its broad doors, which, when opened onto the garden, redefined the shed as a garden pavilion.[13]

The range of Lihotzky's New Frankfurt designs gives an excellent overview of her life's work, and a method that remained fundamentally unchanged over the subsequent decades. In regions as far-flung as Central Europe, the USSR and Turkey, she produced many more examples of kitchens, classrooms, laundries, and the like, in newly modernizing nations.

By 1930, the New Frankfurt initiative was crumbling under political and economic pressure. Lihotzky and her husband Wilhelm Schütte joined Ernst May and fifteen other designers to form the 'May Brigade' and travelled to the Soviet Union to assist in the construction of new cities. The brigade spent the next seven years designing cities—most notably in Magnitogorsk—and much that went with them: the schools, housing, day care centres and the like. They lived in a group house in Moscow, then in barracks on remote construction sites. Their projects were scattered across Russia's vast reaches, such that the team never

12

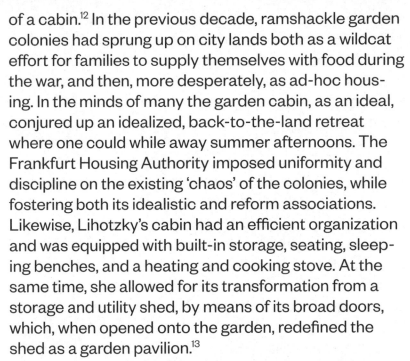

Margarete Schütte-Lihotzky, design for Frankfurt garden cabin, 1927.

13
Susan R. Henderson, *Building Culture: Ernst May and the Frankfurt Initiative, 1926–1932*, Studies in Modern European History 64 (New York etc.: Peter Lang, 2013), pp. 266–75.

saw many of its works. Lihotzky designed housing along with the others, but her primary contribution was in the area of schools, kindergartens and nurseries. It would be the primary focus of her work from here on, and, looking back over her career, this work mattered the most to her.

The first of these was a proposed, though unbuilt, kindergarten for the settlement of Praunheim in Frankfurt. Many more were to follow, though most were either not built or have been lost. The primary record rests in her archive.[14] The primary concern of this work was the creation of a healthy environment: broad windows let in the sunlight, terraces and lawns were there for play, and small gardens introduced children to life cycles, showers and bathing facilities improved hygiene, and kitchens supplied milk and healthy meals. Lihotzky considered a facility in Bryansk in the Ukraine one of her best works. Its two long wings occupied the crest of a hilltop, one wing looking out to the east and, the other west from continuous window walls and balconies. Typical of so much building during the pre-Second World War years, it was destroyed with little remaining but a few photographs of lost renderings. What innovations were surely introduced in the interior layout and equipment are difficult to assess given the meagre documentation. But there are numerous plans and renderings of similar projects, including her Praunheim Kindergarten Frankfurt (1928), a nursery in Magnitogorsk, USSR (1931), two lines of modular furniture for children designed for the Soviet market in the mid-1930s, and a nursery in Sofia, Bulgaria (1946) as part of a larger home economics complex, and a number of later projects in Vienna.

In 1940, after a two-year sojourn in Turkey, Lihotzky determined to join the communist resistance to fascism, and with two collaborators she returned

14
Lihotzky's archive in the collections of the Museum für angewandte Kunst in Vienna. Much of the work is reproduced in the catalogue by Peter Noever et al., eds., *Margarete Schütte-Lihotzky: Soziale Architektur: Zeitzeugin eines Jahrhunderts* (Vienna: Böhlau Verlag, 1996); an Italian version of the same is Lorenza Minoli et al., eds. *Dalla cucina alla cittá: Margarete Schütte-Lihotzky* (Milan: FrancoAngeli, 1999).

Susan R. Henderson

to Vienna as part of the underground. The three were soon captured, and the Gestapo sentenced Lihotzky to fifteen years imprisonment, and executed her collaborators. She served four and a half years before liberation by the Americans. Peacetime Austria did not thank her for her sacrifices, or harness her considerable design expertise. To her chagrin, an ever energetic, now mid-life, Lihotzky found herself excluded from municipal work for refusing to join the Socialist Party. Instead of participating in the reconstruction of her own city, she spent much of the next twenty-five years doing what she called her 'political work'. She belonged to and served as president of the Bund demokratischer Frauen (Union of Democratic Women) from 1947 through 1969. In this work she also acted as a kind of unofficial design ambassador to the Communist Bloc. In 1937, she and husband Wilhelm had spent six weeks advising Chiang Kai-shek on the construction of schools and nurseries. In the post-war period, she made a veritable tour of Communist Bloc countries, lending her expertise to the cause. From Sofia, Bulgaria in 1947, to Mao's China in 1956; Moscow in 1958; in 1961 and 1963 she made a sojourn to Fidel Castro's Cuba advising him on building children's facilities, a visit ending just days before the Bay of Pigs incident; to East Berlin in 1966. It was only in the mid-1980s that she became a celebrated and recognized figure in Vienna, and the subject of many conferences, exhibitions and celebrations.

Margarete Schütte-Lihotzky's career stands as a case study of the ways in which design can serve reform initiatives, and, indeed, the pitfalls and dangers of such a 'praxis' as opposed to, say, careerism. In looking at the history of modernism, one can discern one of the major divides among its advocates as that between designers for whom design was primarily an art form, and those who were politically motivated, and dedicated to the 'ordinary', i.e. the everyday fabric of the house, the street, and social infrastructure. It is to this second group that Lihotzky belongs, to a cohort whose work is marked by a simplicity in which authorship is often virtually impossible to distinguish. This approach to the everyday environment, whereby efficiency of movement in household labour, and space-saving in construction enable a more democratic distribution of resources. Secondly, the social theory of modern life, which coalesced around workers housing, schools, and childcare facilities, aimed to improve and invent an appropriate and humane way of life for the new urban working classes.

One consequence of the split between the proponents of design as an art, and those with a dedication to the everyday and a political and social agenda has been the diminishment of the achievements of the latter group in subsequent histories. Ernst May, Lihotzky herself, Hans Schmidt, Mart Stam, Franz Schuster, all members of the May design team in Frankfurt and/or the Soviet Union, have faded from view in favour of a hall of fame of celebrated architects and designers from the Bauhaus, for example, whose work placed on an emphasis on style and form. At the same time, and in a very real sense, the work of the 'everyday' architects was highly productive towards their stated goal of improving the life of the working class. Among them, Margarete Schütte-Lihotzky remains a particularly remarkable and instructive figure.

Susan R. Henderson

Good Design for Everyone
Scarcity, Equality, and Utility in the Second World War

Marjanne van Helvert

The Second World War was an unlikely time for a social design experiment. In a worldwide crisis, the government of the United Kingdom decided to support a socialist idea to make sure its population would not only be fed, but also properly housed and dressed to make it through the war years. Known as the Utility Scheme, the concept was based on a utopian idea of providing good design for the masses, and educating them on modern living in the process. Although the programme was born out of material scarcity, it has much to offer to conceptions of wicked design problems today.

Scarcity Today

Scarcity is an ambiguous concept. It is most commonly associated with something negative, as in a shortage or lack of desired items or necessary materials. It may be due to poverty, unequal distribution of wealth, corruption, or the depletion of natural resources. It can also occur when the supply chain of products and materials is temporarily disrupted, because of political crises such as war and boycotts, or natural disasters such as floods or earthquakes. Yet the notion of scarcity is also applied, more manipulatively, in capitalist consumer culture and marketing strategies. It is the very concept on which the attractiveness of limited editions and exclusive brands is based. In these instances, scarcity is introduced on purpose to make a product or service more desirable, precisely because it is designed to be rare and only available to the few lucky insiders.[1]

Lately, scarcity has been associated with the imminent exhaustion of fossil fuels and numerous raw materials and minerals that are essential to our industries. Then there is the rapid decline in biodiversity, as countless species of plants and animals and their habitats

1

THE DESIGN OF SCARCITY

GOODBUN, KLEIN, RUMPFHUBER & TILL

For an analysis of the many faces of scarcity, both in design and in economy, see: Jon Goodbun et al., *The Design of Scarcity* (London: Strelka Press, 2014).

Marjanne van Helvert

MAKE DO

MEND AND

are disappearing, some of which we depend on for our own survival. The gradual shifts in the equilibrium of ecosystems and disruptions of climatic patterns are transforming our environment as we know it, and we cannot yet fully predict their consequences for our future well-being. At the same time, the economic crisis of 2008 has brought financial hardship on many. It has led governments to implement policies of austerity that steadily chip away at the welfare states in many countries, contributing to once again inclining rates of poverty, housing issues, and homelessness. A widening gap between the rich and the poor, on both a global and local scale, leaves us in the paradoxical position of being confronted with scarcity and overproduction at the same time.

The idea of shortages stands in sharp contrast with much of our lived experience amid the abundance of stuff we have created, among the masses of cheap products that are offered to us on a daily basis. It seems that we can purchase a limitless amount of gadgets and clothes, take unlimited air trips, and forever eat the last pieces of tuna. Even the markets that the western, industrialized world never before associated with excess, such as places in sub-Saharan Africa, are now flooded with the second-hand leftovers of the fast fashion industry, for example. The fact that we have trouble imagining the massive amounts of waste and pollution that our consumer culture brings forth—as well as our slow recognition of the necessity of recycling and waste reduction—is tantamount to our reluctance to see harm in this system of overproduction.

To people living in the industrialized countries scarcity may connote a rather dystopian idea of the future. For many designers it is hard to imagine having material shortages affecting their work, or missing a consumer base to market their products to. Most designers are accustomed to functioning within the system of over-production where they have to work hard to find a place for their product amidst the abundance of commodities. However, in practice, contemporary policies of waste reduction show interesting parallels to working in circumstances of scarcity. In both instances, designers and producers try to do more with less.

Obviously, for the majority of people in the world scarcity is a very real issue with which they are confronted in some form or other in their daily lives. It is a concept that is intrinsically connected to inequality, as the poor are affected by shortages sooner and on a much more fundamental level than the wealthy. Any attempt at a solution to material scarcity and shortages should acknowledge this and consider a redistribution of resources as well. The Utility Scheme anticipated the connection between scarcity and economic inequality, and was an attempt to unify all actors in the commodity network, including designers, in order to provide a rigorous solution in a time of crisis.

War Socialism

In the Second World War scarcity suddenly became part of the daily lives of every upper, middle and working class citizen in the countries involved. Because of disrupted trade routes, the supply of resources was severely limited. Moreover, the war industry demanded that the majority of materials go into the manufacture of weapons, uniforms, and transportation vehicles, while workers and factories were assigned to produce for the military instead of the consumer market. There were immediate shortages of raw materials such as wood, metal, rubber, cotton, wool and silk, and as the war industry was prioritized, scarcity was most acute

Marjanne van Helvert

in consumer goods. Prices of new and second-hand products rose drastically as retailers and manufacturers ran out of stock.

The United Kingdom had experienced how scarcity affected people with lower incomes in particular, during the First World War. Therefore, following food rationing in January 1940, the British government introduced price control and then the rationing of many consumer goods. The rationing of clothing began in June 1941 and would last until 1952, some years after the war had ended and most scarcity issues were resolved. As rationing alone proved insufficient to solve the shortages and price raises, a comprehensive plan was devised to make sure that enough clothes would be available for the entire population. The clothing plan was part of the Utility Scheme, which also included footwear, furniture, crockery and other daily goods such as pencils and cigarette lighters.[2] It was planned, organized and controlled by the British Board of Trade, which installed and worked closely together with several commissions comprised of people from the industry and the state. During the war years, the Board of Trade reorganized the complete process of production and consumption of these consumer goods. This allowed the Board to control the allocation and distribution of raw materials, the quality and the designs of products, the manufacture by a selected number of firms spread across the country, the local distribution of goods, and the retail to customers with permits to buy certain products. Most of the furniture was reserved for newlyweds and for 'bombees', people whose homes had been destroyed by air raids. Clothing was rationed[3] for everyone and could only be bought with coupons that were issued by the state.

While wartime scarcity affected everyone, the Utility programme provided affordable goods to those

2
Mike Brown, *CC41 Utility Clothing: The Label That Transformed British Fashion* (Sevenoaks: Sabrestorm Publishing, 2014), p. 5.

3

The clothes allowed for one woman a year in Britain, AP Photo, 1940.

4

Julie Summers, *Fashion on the Ration: Style in the Second World War* (London: Profile Books, 2015), p. 5.

5

Brown, *CC41 Utility Clothing*, p. 8.

6

Utility Furniture and Fashion: 1941–1951 (London: Geffrye Museum, 1974), p. 6.

7

A page from the Utility Furniture catalog, 1943.

8

Matthew Denney, 'Utility Furniture and the Myth of Utility 1943–48', in *Utility Reassessed: The Role of Ethics in the Practice of Design*, ed. Judy Attfield (Manchester: Manchester UP, 1999), pp. 110–24.

who really needed them. This meant that many of the poorest people had the opportunity to purchase a new set of good quality clothing for the first time in their lives.[4] While this type of socialist policy was commended by some, others saw it only as a temporary form of crisis management. It was part of the idea that the British people had to be coaxed into supporting the war in every way possible. Posters and advertisements urged them to knit socks for the troops, to 'make do' and mend the things they had so these would last longer, to save fuel, and even to not dress too extravagantly, because that implied an unpatriotic waste of material and labour. The war socialism of the Utility Scheme was part of the support for the 'total war', and therefore even the more conservative politicians backed it for the time being.[5]

The intentions of the Board of Trade, however, were very broad. It was not only concerned with supplying the bare necessities to those in need, but aimed to produce good quality products for everyone. These goods were to be made with as little material and labour as possible, and according to what its advisors considered principles of good design.[6] As opposed to providing only a cheap, temporary solution, Utility products were made to be durable and modern, in an attempt to educate the public in modern taste. The furniture was inspired by Arts and Crafts as well as modernist design,[7] but the unadorned, functionalist pieces were also simply intended to save material and production time.[8] The design of clothing and furniture was standardized and centralized for efficiency, which meant that the manufacturers themselves were not required to have their own internal design departments anymore, as they had to produce whatever the designers of the Board prescribed. Strict rules were imposed to make sure that no material or labour was wasted in the process. Even fuel

Marjanne van Helvert

for transportation was saved as much as possible by the careful planning of the supply chain in which manufacturers and retailers were evenly spread across the country.

CC41: Utility Fashion

The clothing that was produced under the Utility Scheme was labelled with the recognizable 'CC41' mark.[9] 41 stood for the year in which it was introduced; CC meant either nothing in particular, or stood for 'civilian clothing' or 'controlled commodity', according to different sources.[10] The Utility designs were characterized by straight lines, a slim silhouette and little or no embellishment. The women's clothes tended to be practical and were influenced by the look of uniforms, anticipating the different roles that women fulfilled during the war. To save material, unnecessary pleats were not allowed, and neither were double breasted jackets and long socks for men. Things like buttons, buckles, zippers, and elastic were limited because metal and rubber were needed for the war industry. Skirts were to be knee-length, coats were kept short, and boys under thirteen were not allowed to wear long trousers. Extra pockets were discarded, as were decorative elements such as embroidery, appliqué or lace. Men's suits had small collars, no flaps over the pockets of the jacket, no turn-ups on the bottoms of trousers, no slits and buttons on the cuffs. Colours, however, were not restricted. Fabric prints for dresses for example were often small, busy patterns of colourful flowers[11] that were easy to put together without having to waste fabric to make the motif connect. The Board of Trade estimated that all of these regulations saved millions of meters of cloth.

9

Label with the CC41 Utility mark designed by Reginald Shipp, 1941.

10

Summers, *Fashion on the Ration*, p. 96; Brown, *CC41 Utility Clothing*, p. 31.

11

Flower print M&S Utility fabric, 1940s.

12
Jonathan Walford, *Forties Fashion: From Siren Suits to the New Look* (London: Thames & Hudson, 2008), p. 49.

13

Norman Hartnell, Utility clothing designs, 1943.

14
Summers, *Fashion on the Ration*, pp. 103–5.

15

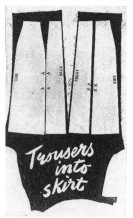

Recycling tutorial from wartime magazine showing how to make a skirt from an old pair of men's trousers, 1940s.

16

As one would expect, not everyone was convinced that austerity measures and fashion would go well together. The name Utility did not help, as it conveyed a sense of drab uniforms or purely functional clothing that had nothing to do with fashion. Since both the trade and the British public were initially apprehensive of the Utility Scheme, the Board of Trade invited well-known designers of the time to design a range of items, including a top coat, dress, blouse, skirt and suit.[12] Well-known couturiers Norman Hartnell,[13] Digby Morton, Bianca Mosca, Elspeth Champcommunal, Edward Molyneux, Peter Russell, Charles Creed and Victor Stiebel had formed the Incorporated Society of London Fashion Designers (IncSoc) to promote British fashion, and were asked to contribute designs to what came to be known as the couturier scheme. The involvement of these esteemed designers and the favourable reports their work received from magazines such as *Vogue* and *Harper's Bazaar*, helped promote Utility clothing to the public. Retailers initially complained that the couturier designs were too fancy and not practical for everyday wear, but they did change the idea of Utility fashion. Because of the low prices and good quality, and sometimes simply because they were the only thing available, Utility clothes became well appreciated.[14]

Aside from the few new garments that one could buy on coupons, the people were urged and often had no other choice than to endlessly repair, recycle and share whatever was available. The British government issued leaflets with instructions on how to repair damaged textiles and how to alter clothes. There were items on how to line coats with pieces of recycled textile to make them warmer for the winter, for example; how to fashion a jacket and skirt out of an old men's suit,[15] and how to enlarge children's clothing when it became too small.[16] There were many ways in which people tried to

16 (cont.)
See for example: *Make Do and Mend: Keeping Family and Home Afloat on War Rations*. London: Michael O'Mara, 2007. This is a book of reproductions of official Second World War instruction leaflets.

Marjanne van Helvert

be creative with what was afforded to them. Anyone who could sew would make their own clothes, as many people still did at the time. However, as new fabrics were equally scarce or expensive, other materials, such as furnishing fabrics, curtains, bed sheets, and blackout cloth were used. Children's clothes made of pillow cases or blouses made of handkerchiefs were not uncommon. As natural and artificial silks were much sought after, parachute nylon sometimes proved an acceptable substitute material for making wedding dresses or lingerie.

The Second World War was a time when, in the absence of the men who were in military service, large numbers of women went to work outside the home in professions that were previously not available to them. Many women wore uniforms while working shifts in hospitals or in transportation, or donned overalls in the factories. Faced with the limited choices in civilian clothing as well, women expressed their style and femininity with creative accessories, and hairdos. Hats were popular but expensive, and elaborate hairstyles formed a decent alternative. Women also tied up their hair with scarves for practical reasons while working, or rolled them into extravagant turbans for extra flair. When makeup was in short supply, some used beetroot as a substitute for lipstick and shoe polish for mascara. Magazines urged women to keep up appearances, as it was argued to be bad for the public morale if women would abandon traditionally feminine looks.

The Aftermath

The Utility programme not only had a big influence on what people were able to buy and wear during the war, it also changed how products were manufactured.

17
Brown, *CC41 Utility Clothing*, p. 44.

Before the war, the clothing industry was still largely in the hands of local tailors and dressmakers. The Board of Trade, however, intended to make the chain of production as efficient as possible. Out of the firms that applied to become designated Utility producers, which was an attractive position because it guaranteed commissions, the Board chose the larger, more modern factories over smaller, traditional companies and tradespeople, since they could produce more and faster with less labour.[17] In doing so, the Utility program contributed to the stimulation of mass-production, which was of course soon to accelerate on a much larger scale.

Scarcity issues were not resolved immediately when the war ended. Demands for clothing increased, for example, because during demobilization soldiers were returning home and needed to replace their uniforms with civilian clothes. There was also a difference of perception between the political right and left as to what post-war society should look like. The conservatives wanted to end war socialism as soon as possible, while the Labour party, winning the first post-war election in 1945, recognized it as part of the welfare state, which also included the establishment of the National Health Service and Universal Child Benefits at the time. In 1951 the political tide changed when the conservatives won the election with the slogan 'Set the People Free'. The Utility clothing programme gradually relaxed its regulations and prescriptions over the years and ended completely in 1952.

Right after the war, in Paris in 1947, fashion designer Christian Dior debuted a collection that was soon dubbed the 'New Look'. It would come to be celebrated in the next decade of women's fashion. Characterized by long, full skirts with padded hips, tiny waists, and close fitting bodices, his dresses were nostalgically

Marjanne van Helvert

inspired by the corseted gowns of the previous century. They were quite the opposite of the subdued silhouette of the practical Utility clothes that had reigned during the austerity years. This new style implied a complete regression of the role of women in society, which at the time was advocated by many reactionary voices that wished them to return to a life of domestic service. Although there was initially some controversy surrounding the extravagance of the look in a time that was still dominated by shortages, both the press and the public soon embraced it.[18] They were eager for something new and spectacular after those ascetic years of make-do. It could seem that this stylistic counter-reaction undid the changes that happened in dressing habits during the war, but along with the next steps in the emancipation of women and the slowly diminishing class divisions that followed, Utility fashion anticipated the more egalitarian and universal clothing customs that developed in the second half of the century.

Good Design for Good Living

The idea of good design for everyone persisted for some time after the war, especially in regard to furniture design. In 1949, Gordon Russell, Chairman of the Utility Design Panel, published his article 'What is Good Design?', in which he argued that good design 'is an essential part of a standard of quality' and 'always takes into account the technique of production, the material to be used, and the purpose for which the object is wanted'.[19] His functionalist conception of design stood in a tradition of modernist and socialist ideals of providing all citizens with decent housing and furniture, which can also be found in the principles of the Arts & Crafts movement, the Deutscher Werkbund and the Bauhaus,

18
Julian Robinson, *Fashion in the 40s* (New York: St. Martin's, 1980), p. 55.

19
Gordon Russell, 'What Is Good Design?', *Design* 1 (January 1949), pp. 2–6, www.vads.ac.uk/learning/designingbritain/pdf/crd_2.pdf.

for example. In all of these instances the idea of good design was connected to the endeavour to elevate working class people from slums and educate them on better hygiene and 'good taste'. Russell argued that 'a public which possesses critical standards is essential if design is to be as good as it might be'.[20] The circumstances of the war provided Russell and like-minded designers with the opportunity to put these ideals into practice.

20
Russell, 'What Is Good Design?', p. 5.

After the Second World War, a large number of social housing estates were established in Europe and in other parts of the world. Many of these housing projects adopted largescale modernist plans to deal with the urgency of housing a growing urban population and rebuilding the cities after the destruction of war. Modernist ideals were applied to the recommended interiors as well. In the Netherlands, for example, an organization called Goed Wonen (Good Living) published a magazine on modern interiors, and set up model apartments[21] in the new post-war neighbourhoods in Amsterdam, in which future inhabitants were invited to learn what were considered the right and the wrong choices in decorating their new homes. The interiors that were displayed had plain white walls, and contained light, often multifunctional modern furniture that contrasted greatly with the upholstered oak furniture, flower-patterned wallpaper and heavy curtains that most people preferred at the time. The steel furniture of the Bauhaus was an inspiration for Goed Wonen, but since metal was scarce after the war, it was substituted with wood and rattan. According to Goed Wonen, modern furniture presupposed more ease in cleaning the house, as it was easier to move and had a minimum of upholstery, making it less dusty. The general openness and plainness of the modern interior was said to afford a more efficient use of space, and promoted their ideals

21

Goed Wonen model interior, 1956, photo by Arjé Plas. Collection Van Eesterenmuseum.

Marjanne van Helvert

of 'light, air, and linoleum'.[22] Goed Wonen also issued a mark of approval to companies they considered to be examples of good design, such as Gispen and Pastoe, in a way quite similar to the Utility mark.

  The promotion of 'good design' took on different forms around the world. In Germany there was the similar idea of 'good form' for example, conceptualized in different ways by the Deutscher Werkbund and the Hochschule für Gestaltung Ulm. Although the majority of the public tended to find modern design too austere, and gladly held on to their preferred reproduction furniture and flower patterns, these discussions on design did establish a new idea of what was considered good taste. In the United States of America, in 1950, an exhibition series with the title 'Good Design'[23] was organized by the Museum of Modern Art in New York City and the Merchandise Mart, a retail and wholesale company in Chicago. It featured pieces by Marcel Breuer, Eero Saarinen, Hans Wegner, and Charles and Ray Eames who also designed the inaugural installation, as well as everyday objects such as kitchen ware, tools and textiles. It established an idea of what good design was supposed to look like that lingers to this day. Yet many iconic pieces in the exhibition did not end up in working or middle class homes, but became status symbols instead.

Political or Design Choices

The extreme measures that were taken by the British state to cope with scarcity issues during the Second World War might seem incompatible with today's market capitalism and consumer society. The control that was exercised over the design of consumer goods appears quite paternalistic in a world where the consum-

22
A series of books about the post-war 'Garden Cities' of Amsterdam contains photos of contemporary interiors of the inhabitants of these modernist apartments, compared to the model apartments of Goed Wonen. For example: Ineke Teijmant and Bart Sorgedrager, *De Verfdoos 1956–2009* (Amsterdam: Lubberhuizen, 2010).

23

'Good Design' exhibition at MoMA New York, photo by Soichi Sunami, 1951.

er's choice reigns as the hallmark of the free market. In the material crisis that came with the war, an attempt was made to transform capitalist consumer culture into a closed, national system that provided good quality, modern commodities on the basis of material equality. The British government was able to turn a material crisis into a temporarily rather successful solution. It took control over the total functioning of the commodity network, determining the fate of designers, manufacturers, and retailers alike, some of whom were put out of work or were forced to radically change their practices. After the war these rules were quickly reversed, to the relief of many. Yet in its deliberate connection between material scarcity and socio-economic inequality, the Utility Scheme does offer an alternative perspective on the complexity of contemporary issues. Today it is often assumed that the market will take care of solving our problems, whether they are environmental, social or economic. Yet, so far, the majority of commercial design and technological innovation has not been deployed to target the long-term challenges humanity is facing, but is instead actively engaged in aggravating them. The Utility Scheme shows that in a time of acute crisis, it is necessary to not only look at the design and production of scarce goods, but to also reconsider the political, economic and social systems and conventions that surround them.

Marjanne van Helvert

DESIGN AS TERRAIN

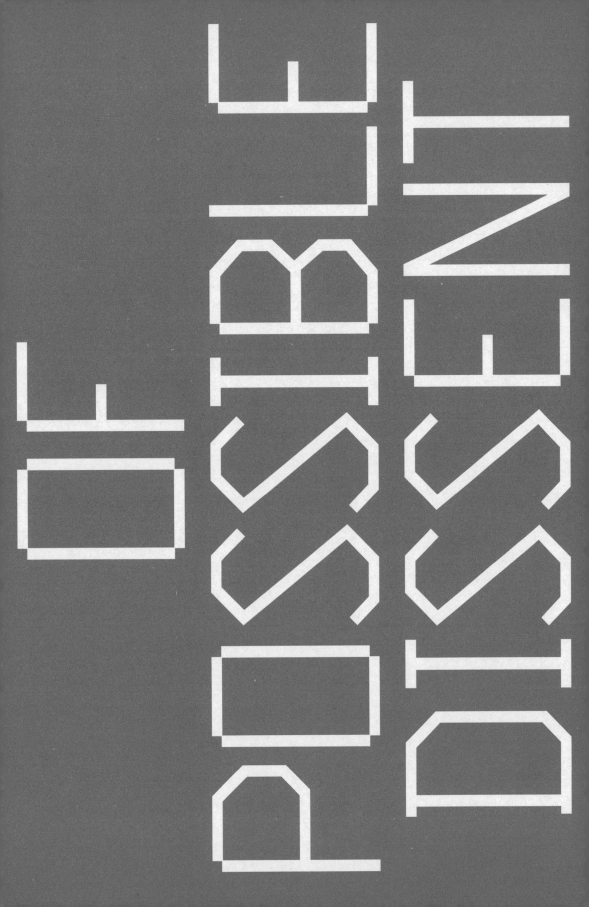

OF POSSIBLE DISSENT

Design for Consumer Society
Planned Obsolescence, Styling, and Irresponsible Objects

Marjanne van Helvert

Although many elements had already fallen into place in previous decades, consumer society came into full swing in the 1950s, first in North America and later also in Western Europe and other countries around the world. Industrial design became its celebrated partner. The most famous European designers of the first half of the twentieth century had often incorporated socialist principles in their work, with the utopian intent to change the lives of the population for the better through design. After the Second World War a new age of consumerism, advertising, and styling took over, as the market increasingly dictated design decisions. Design became primarily a means to sell a product, rather than improve it. With a growing middle class and a booming economy, North America became the centre of commercial design, and offered designers the opportunity to become stars. While much of the world was trying to rebuild both its economy and its morale, North American consumer culture and its products were exported to Western Europe as a result of the Marshall Plan, and with similar post-war American subsidy programmes worldwide. The financial aid that the European, Asian and Middle Eastern countries received, was often spent directly on US products, boosting the United States' economy and spreading its material and ideological influence around the world.

There is no clear break between the more socially committed designers of the first half of the twentieth century and the more commercially inspired design of the second half. Yet the inter- and post-war years provide many examples that illustrate the increasing influence of the consumer capitalist system on design, and thus the involvement of industrial design in supporting an unsustainable production and consumption culture. Many of the characteristics of today's consumer society were solidified during this time, while much

Marjanne van Helvert

of the criticism it currently receives already started to be voiced as well. Much social and sustainable design, both today and in the past, appears to challenge characteristics of consumer society as we know it, such as the ubiquity of disposable objects, the careless use of precious materials, or the harsh labour conditions under which many of our commodities are produced. These unsustainable practices have become part of daily reality to such an extent that we take them for granted, as if they have always been part of our design and consumption system, which makes it difficult to recognize and challenge them. It is therefore useful to deconstruct some of the characteristics of consumer society, such as obsolescence and styling, in which design plays a major part. A historical perspective reveals that these practices have not always been as self-evident as they now appear to be, and have been heavily criticized in the past as well.

Planned Obsolescence

At a fire station in Livermore, California, hangs the world's oldest lightbulb. It has been burning faithfully and almost without interruption since 1901. Nicknamed the Centennial Light, it is cared for by the Centennial Light Bulb Committee, which celebrated its hundredth birthday in 2001. It has its own website where you can see it in action twenty-four hours a day via its own webcam.[1] The reason that people find this old light bulb so amazing is that we are not used to products lasting that long. Most people in industrialized countries live in a culture of disposables, ranging from paper cups that last one coffee break, clothes that last a season, to laptops which last a few years before they become too slow and we replace them. While we can usually design

1
www.centennialbulb.org.

and save up for better products, that could serve us a lifetime or could even be passed on to our children and grandchildren, both designers and consumers regularly choose not to do so, for many different reasons.

The Centennial Light is often mentioned in discussions around 'planned obsolescence', as its remarkable lifespan seems to disagree with our current conception of the longevity of light bulbs.[2] Planned obsolescence is the concept of designing and producing commodities with the intention of giving them an artificially limited lifespan. This can be achieved, for example, by working with low quality materials or by using inferior production methods. It is a complex concept that is deeply ingrained within capitalist society and within design.

This particular light bulb was produced by the Shelby Electric Company in Ohio at the end of the nineteenth century. There are quite a few of those very old, still working bulbs around, while modern light bulbs are known to expire within a few years of use. The technological prowess in light bulb production almost seems to have taken some steps backwards a century later. In 1924, a group of light bulb manufacturers consisting of Osram, Philips and General Electric, among others, formed a cartel in an effort to take control of their trade. They came up with a new plan to respond to declining sales. The companies agreed that from then on they would only produce light bulbs that were designed to last a maximum of 1000 hours, even though they were capable of producing more durable ones. This meant that the manufacturers could use cheaper materials and produce more bulbs at lower costs, and also that their customers would have to keep purchasing new bulbs as they burned out over the years. The customer had no choice but to buy the lesser product, since the manufacturers had banded together and therefore there was no competition. While there may have

2
See for example the documentary *The Light Bulb Conspiracy*, directed by Cosima Dannoritzer, 2010.

Marjanne van Helvert

also been a technical imperative to the agreement, as longer-lasting incandescent light bulbs are found to be less energy efficient, the cartel established a successful way of selling more products. It has been copied endlessly thereafter. Planned obsolescence might now be seen by environmentalists as a disastrous invention, but in the depression era when it was conceived, it was considered a necessary and successful interference with declining sales. As such, planned obsolescence was believed to help restore the economy, to keep factories running, and thus provide much-needed jobs.[3] After the depression, it was kept in place in many parts of the industry as a way to guarantee continuous sales.

Besides purposely designing and producing goods with low quality standards, planned obsolescence has also been achieved by deliberately dispensing with the option to adapt, repair and update products. This has become a dominant convention in consumer electronics. When our electronic devices break down or become slow we tend to replace the whole device, rather than just the worn or broken element, as this is often cheaper than having it repaired. Most of us do not have the knowledge to perform repairs ourselves. Additionally, it is sometimes impossible to obtain replacement parts, and many devices cannot even be opened up. The conventional design of electronic devices has become surface design, which is characterized by impenetrable polished exteriors behind which the mechanisms and electronics are stored away. Yet this was not always the case.

In *Objects of Desire: Design and Society 1750–1980*, design historian Adrian Forty describes how domestic appliances, such as kitchen mixers or radios, transformed from being very functionalistic and industrial-looking with visible mechanisms and wires, to being wrapped in smooth, white plastic coverings in the

3
For more on planned obsolescence in the depression era, see the 1932 paper by Bernard London, 'Ending the Depression Through Planned Obsolescence', Wikimedia, upload.wikimedia.org/wikipedia/commons/2/27/London_(1932)_Ending_the_depression_through_planned_obsolescence.pdf (accessed 10 April, 2016).

1950s. As the first electric equipment that appeared in the early twentieth century was expensive and meant to be operated by servants, the industrial look was no problem. The new domestic machines were basically smaller scale copies of industrial ones.[4] After the war, however, appliances were increasingly mass-produced, became cheaper, and were consequently marketed towards middle and lower class households as well. There, the housewife was expected to take care of domestic work, which was implied to be an elevated situation compared to working outside the home in a factory, for example. Forty argues that the consumer did not want to be reminded of industrial labour when operating a vacuum cleaner or a washing machine, and this was the prime reason that the design of many household products underwent a significant transformation. Appliance design became dominated by a sealed-off surface aesthetic, where the polished, often white exterior of the product concealed the functional elements inside. The machine became boxed up in a shell with only a few buttons or knobs to operate it, so that it looked simpler and less intimidating to the consumer. The German company Braun,[5] and its well-known designers Hans Gugelot and Dieter Rams, were very influential in pioneering this convention, and other companies soon followed in their footsteps.[6]

These surface aesthetics continue to dominate consumer electronics to this day, and they reinforce the assumption that the object should not and cannot be opened up. Users are not supposed to interfere with the mechanics of the machine, as they are not expected to understand its workings. In more recent times, technology company Apple, whose head designer Jonathan Ive is a known Rams fan, is one of the many companies that have been accused of employing this type of policy in order to limit the lifespan of its products. Well-known

Advertisement for Kitchen Aid mixer, 1920s.

Gerd Alfred Müller, Braun KM3 kitchen mixer, 1957.

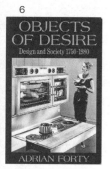

Adrian Forty, *Objects of Desire* (New York: Pantheon Books, 1986), pp. 215-20.

Marjanne van Helvert

examples are the iPod, whose battery inevitably loses capacity over time, but is irreplaceable,[7] and the Retina MacBook Pro, which has been named the 'least-repairable' notebook ever.[8] It is glued together to save weight, making it impossible to open up to replace parts or carry out repairs. Some devices are even programmed to stop functioning after a certain time. Hewlett Packard for example has been sued by its customers for using programmed obsolescence. The company was accused of programming the chips in its ink cartridges to communicate to the printer that they needed to be replaced when they were in fact still half full.[9]

Styling and Restyling

Another type of planned obsolescence, and one that seems almost too obvious to be named as such, is styling. An early example of it being purposely used to promote obsolescence can be found in the history of the car industry. Around the same time that the light bulb cartel was formed, the car industry in the United States faced a saturation of the market. Everyone who could afford one had a car now, so the major growth of the previous decades was over. Some car manufacturers decided to try a new sales tactic. It was a different one than the deal of the light bulb companies, but it had a similar effect. After having produced one model car successfully for many years, they introduced new styles. Styling became a way to market a new car which essentially only had a new exterior, covering the exact same technology underneath. This way, new models could be introduced over and over again, in an attempt to convince the consumer that they always needed to replace their car for a more fashionable one.[10] Needless to say, it was a huge success.[11]

7
Hank Stuever, 'Battery And Assault', *The Washington Post*, 20 December 2003, www.washingtonpost.com/archive/lifestyle/2003/12/20/battery-and-assault/29056cfd-59d7-4dc7-b12f-cda99203ae6d (accessed 25 April, 2016).

8
Kyle Wiens, 'The New MacBook Pro: Unfixable, Unhackable, Untenable', *Wired* 14 June 2012, www.wired.com/2012/06/opinion-apple-retina-displa (accessed 25 April 2016).

9
Daniel DiClerico, 'HP Inkjet Printer Lawsuit Reaches $5 Million Settlement', *Consumer Reports*, 17 November 2010, www.consumerreports.org/cro/news/2010/11/hp-inkjet-printer-lawsuit-reaches-5-million-settlement/index.htm (accessed 25 April 2016).

10

Advertisement for a Chevrolet Utility coupé, 1923.

11
For more on obsolescence and styling see: Giles Slade, *Made to Break: Technology and Obsolescence in America* (Cambridge: Harvard University Press, 2006).

Today, styling is so much part of our culture and of the job of many a designer that we perceive it as a given. It is something that implies progress, novelty, and sophistication, highly valued qualities in our society. The most obvious and successful example of styling happens in the way we dress ourselves, as the word fashion, a synonym of style, has even come to denominate the clothing industry as a whole. Most of the time, we buy new clothes not because all of our old ones have worn out, but because we do not want to appear out of style. High fashion labels have been turning out new collections faster and faster over the past decades, going from two, to four, to six collections a year. Fast fashion giants like Zara, H&M, and Primark introduce sub-collections throughout the seasons, so that their customers see something new in the stores every few weeks. These clothing chains are known for not really designing clothes themselves, but rather taking their cues from the catwalks. They have become experts at copying catwalk trends and transforming them into mass-produced items that hit the stores within a matter of weeks. Due to their low material quality, fast fashion clothes do need to be replaced often because they wear out, as they are only intended to function for one season.

Irresponsible Objects

Mid twentieth century, a specific form of styling became the symbol of criticism of this custom. It was the iconic streamlining trend, which started in the 1930s and continued well into the 1950s. Aesthetically related to Art Deco, architects and industrial designers applied seamless, aerodynamic forms to not only cars and trains, where they may have had more than just

Marjanne van Helvert

an aesthetic function, but also to buildings and to objects and appliances[12] such as radios, refrigerators and vacuum cleaners. The designs were often executed in new materials such as aluminum and bakelite, whose smooth shapes with their rounded edges and characteristic horizontal lines fostered a sense of speed, of the future, and of scientific progress. Streamlining became very popular in the United States, and turned some of its associated designers, like Norman Bel Geddes and especially Raymond Loewy, into stars.

Streamlining is most iconically represented by the large American cars that embodied the style in the nineteen-fifties.[13] These cars in particular became the objects of criticism by writers and designers like Vance Packard, Ralph Nader, and Victor Papanek. While American cars became larger and more extravagant with every newly introduced model, the mechanics of the cars were not improved upon. As Victor Papanek stated with obvious disgust in his 1970 best-seller *Design for the Real World*: '...with the primary use function of the automobile solved', the car became 'a combination status symbol and disposable, chrome-plated codpiece'.[14] In 1965, political activist Ralph Nader had published his influential book *Unsafe at Any Speed*, in which he attacked the car industry for the intended and unintended effects of planned obsolescence. He argued that designers and manufacturers only concerned themselves with endlessly renewing the style of the exterior of the car, but that there were hardly any mechanical improvements. He heavily criticized the lack of adequate safety regulations in the car industry, evidenced by an increasing number of fatal traffic accidents.[15] Eventually, Nader's and others' criticisms led to the introduction of mandatory safety checks and features such as safety belts in cars.

Another influential review of American consumer

12

Proctor toaster advertisement, 1948.

13

Advertisement for Buick Roadmaster, 1956.

14

Victor Papanek, *Design for the Real World: Human Ecology and Social Change* (London: Thames & Hudson, 2011), p. 14.

15

15 (cont.)
Ralph Nader, *Unsafe at Any Speed: The Designed-in Dangers of the American Automobile* (New York: Grossman, 1965).

Design for Consumer Society

culture was delivered by the journalist Vance Packard, who throughout his career published widely on various sociological subjects. His 1957 book *The Hidden Persuaders* dealt with the advertising industry, and argued that advertisers and marketing researchers use morally questionable psychological techniques to manipulate the public into thinking it needed to buy products or vote for certain politicians. He argued that advertisers focus on psychological needs, such as emotional security, power, or immortality, and play on the doubts and anxieties due to the lack thereof. Through advertising, consumers are led to believe they can satisfy these needs by purchasing the product.[16] Packard's research continued to foster a distrust in the advertising and marketing world. His next book, *The Status Seekers*, from 1959, analysed socio-economic inequality in the United States. It argued that the capitalist ideal of democratizing prosperity did not equally benefit everyone, and that social classes were kept in place by elites in an effort to consolidate their own wealth.[17]

Packard continued his campaign against the unwanted effects of consumer society with *The Waste Makers*, in 1960. This book was an attack on planned obsolescence, waste, and material inefficiency, which he maintained had become the bedrock of US design and manufacturing of consumer goods. In the chapter 'Planned Obsolescence of Desirability' he argued that planned quality obsolescence, in which products are made to 'wear out or to look shoddy after a few years' did not go fast enough for marketers and producers.[18]

> The safer, more widely applicable approach, many soon concluded, was to wear the product out in the owner's mind. Strip it of its desirability even though it continues to function dutifully.[19]

16
Vance Packard, *The Hidden Persuaders* (New York: D. McKay, 1957).

17
Vance Packard, *The Status Seekers: An Exploration of Class Behavior in America and the Hidden Barriers That Affect You, Your Community, Your Future* (New York: D. McKay, 1959).

18

Vance Packard, *The Waste Makers* (London: Longmans, 1960), p. 68.

19
Ibid.

Marjanne van Helvert

This approach was, of course, styling. Through interviews with product designers and marketing researchers, Packard traced the focus on obsolescence through styling to the precedent of women's fashion which other industries tried to follow: 'In the fifties, designers in a great many fields earnestly studied the obsolescence-creating techniques pioneered in the field of clothing and accessories, particularly those for women.'[20] Through the lowering of prices because of increased mass-production, fashionable dress came within reach of the middle and working classes, and the clothing industry had by then already proven to be enormously successful in convincing them of the need to buy new garments solely because of a newly arrived style. This precedent was adopted by other fields and industries such as consumer electronics, kitchen ware, and furniture, which in turn accelerated their style updates by way of yearly varying colour palettes, ornamentations, and successively changing silhouettes.

The Waste Makers, like Packard's earlier publications, was furiously criticized, as exemplified by a review by A. Edward Miller in the *Journal of Marketing* in 1961:

> These books are all on the wasteful side; the author had an opportunity to perform a useful and constructive service by reporting in proper perspective the complex and admirable way in which the great American distribution system functions. That approach probably would not sell nearly as many copies as the tack which Packard has taken, the shining of a glaring spotlight on the distribution system so that every imperfection—some real and some contrived—is highlighted.[21]

20
Ibid, p. 71.

21
A. Edward Miller, 'Hasty Conclusions About Waste'. Review of *The Waste Makers. Journal of Marketing* 25, no. 4 (1961), p. 109.

22
Ibid., p. 110.

He continued: 'Even the most diabolical marketing man cannot exist on deception, shoddy products, and the kind of waste and inefficiency which Vance Packard claims is the norm.'[22] Miller's reaction echoed a feeling that was and is held by many, as it is broadly accepted that consumer capitalism has brought unprecedented levels of prosperity, and that its flaws of waste and inefficiency are small compared to its gains. While Packard's research certainly has been widely discussed, it cannot be said that its insights really changed our way of designing and consuming. Yet in the light of today's environmental and economic crises, which arguably are the result of a globally extrapolated version of the consumer culture of the fifties, Packard's analyses do take on a new level of urgency. They show us that many of the design conventions that we take for granted today have been ingeniously and artificially constructed in another age, and are therefore not impervious to change. The introduction and acceleration of restyling and other forms of planned obsolescence are norms that can be challenged, and designers ought to be aware of their responsibility in either reaffirming or subverting these conditions in their work. A well-known example of an initiative that attempts to offer an alternative to designing and producing obsolescence is cradle-to-cradle. This concept, popularized by the book of the same title by chemist Michael Braungart and architect William McDonough, promotes design and production that mimics biological processes such as the complete recycling and regeneration of materials in order to arrive at an industry without waste.[23]

The criticisms by Packard, Nader, Papanek, and their followers demonstrated a growing discontent with the perceived effects of consumer culture. Even though the long term consequences of disproportionate CO_2 emissions and other invasive forms of environmental

23

William McDonough and Michael Braungart, *Cradle to Cradle: Remaking the Way We Make Things* (New York: North Point Press, 2002).

Marjanne van Helvert

DO MORE AND
MORE WITH
LESS AND
LESS UNTIL

EVENTUALLY YOU CAN DO EVERYTHING WITH NOTHING

pollution were still largely unknown at the time, their arguments were already centred on challenging some of its causes: a designed overproduction and overconsumption resulting in inefficient and unnecessary waste of materials and energy within consumer society. They saw design as complicit in supporting and reaffirming these systematic conventions, and consequently as a terrain of possible dissent.

The Buckminster Fuller Mission

Ed van Hinte

He was a peculiar man. In the autumn of 1927, Richard Buckminster Fuller, then aged 32, decided to turn his life into an experiment, in order to find out what difference one man could make on a mission to benefit mankind. Now we know that his mindset still has considerable meaning. His unconventional inventions and designs are good examples of truly innovative thinking, and his position on the subservient role of technology should be an inspiration to the sustainability advocates of today.

Fuller's significance for today and for the future does not reveal itself easily. He is not as familiar a figure to the general public as he used to be. His reputation as a true visionary mainly lives within professional circles, particularly among those who have an affinity with mechanical structures and how they look.

Enigmatic

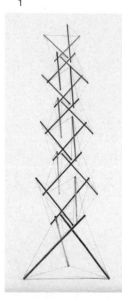

1

On the premises of many an art academy, design school or university department of architecture all over the world, one is likely to encounter some version or other of a 'tensegrity' structure. They quite often resemble abstract sculptures made by Kenneth Snelson,[1] who was one of Buckminster Fuller's students. Objects of that kind are appealing to modernist creators because in a rather enigmatic way they envision the quality of structural transparency, a dogma of contemporary architecture. They consist of struts held together by a cable in perfect balance, without the struts touching each other. Wooden beams or steel pipes seem to freely float in the air, like multidirectional equilibrists. Thousands of pictures are on the Web.

Looks, however, usually distract from the issue at hand. Tensegrity is one of Fuller's most important

Kenneth Snelson, *E.C. Column*, 1969–1990.

Ed van Hinte

discoveries. The word tensegrity, not surprisingly, is a combination of tension and integrity. It roughly means, 'structural integrity based on tension', but in fact it implies a radical separation of tension forces and pressure forces in construction. The advantage is that you can use materials that are good in dealing with either tension, or pressure. Bending, which entails both tension and pressure, is circumvented.

This may sound quite technical, but it is not really complicated, Struts are like columns in temples. They support loads and can deal with pressure and can keep things apart. A slender cable on the other hand is totally incapable of support, but very strong when you hang a weight from it, depending on the material of the cable, of course. For tension then, slenderness is a way of saving material. Focusing on the tension capabilities of cables, wires, or fibres is the key to Richard Buckminster Fuller's thinking, which says: 'Do more and more with less and less until eventually you can do everything with nothing.'[2]

This is similar to 'less is more', an all too often quoted adage of architect Mies van der Rohe. The latter's words, however, refer to simplicity of visual style and not to physical reduction of mass. As a matter of fact the look of 'less is more' may come at a price, that of extra weight. There is more to less than meets the eye.

The visionary Buckminster Fuller firmly believed that beauty was the natural consequence of functionality. That is why, according to him, a rose is beautiful.[3] He never believed in certain aesthetic rules to follow. To him, reduction of physical mass was an inevitable functional development, which he called 'ephemeralization'. He observed that technology was in a process of evolution from compression to tension, to visual, to what he called 'abstract electrical', which is in a sense actually happening. Just think of computer interaction and

2
Ephemeralization, see Wikipedia.

3
'The World of Buckminster Fuller', YouTube video (accessed 1 March 2016).

internet gaming through VR goggles gradually replacing mechanical contraptions. These days, tangible objects have been partly replaced by digital information, which is a more precise expression than 'abstract electrical'. And data are indeed visualized on screens. This implies that the telltale tensegrity signs of Buckminster Fuller-ness in and around design schools can well be seen as illustrations of a principle in transition from compression to tension, which he recognized as such. He tended to think along the lines of counterbalancing forces.

The disadvantage, as announced earlier, is that tensegrity in all these magically empty objects presents itself as an idea just waiting to be applied in a building or a piece of furniture. This has happened occasionally, but there was never really any practical benefit. As a representation of tensegrity all these wonderful strut and cable contraptions are brilliant, but that is as far as it gets: structures for the sake of themselves.

Practical examples of tensegrity certainly do exist and have been around for eons, spontaneously as well as designed, but they are not easily recognizable. They don't look like your tensegrity school examples, for it is not the appearance, but the principle that counts. Look in the mirror and behold: you are a tensegrity structure yourself, consisting of bones to withstand compression caused by gravity, dynamically held together by tendons and muscles, which know how to handle tension well. Or think of a soap bubble. It consists of an amount of air under pressure, held together by a thin film of soapy water that can just about cope with the required tension. Tensegrity even works within plastics that are reinforced, mostly with glass or carbon fibres. They are known as composites and the fibres deal with tension whereas the plastic takes up compression. Fuller pioneered in the application of glass fibre composites,

Ed van Hinte

although it is not clear whether he recognized them as tensegrity structures, or saw them as new materials.

Dymaxion

So principles are what he was looking for: principles plus opportunities to apply them, to save materials and energy, a strategy currently almost neglected. All attention is focused on shifting energy conversion principles from burning fuels to exploiting the sun, and on reuse and recycling, whereas reduction is bound to diminish the need for energy and for reuse and for recycling, or: do more with less.

Apart from his designs, his extremely comprehensive Dymaxion Chronofiles, starting in 1917, testify to his way of reasoning. In these written texts, audiotapes and video recordings he documented his life. Together they form an archive of a baffling 420 metres. Part of it is a 42 hours video series entitled *Everything I Know*. In section 1 of this super interview recording,[4] Buckminster Fuller tells a story that demonstrates the problem-solving eagerness of his designer mind. As a young man he worked as an engineer in the engine room of a navy vessel. At one point he felt he needed to go out for some fresh air and went on deck, all greasy. Outside it was fresh and foggy. After a while he discovered that the fog had an unexpected cleansing effect on his body. Dirt and grease disappeared. He decided to investigate the possibility of developing some kind of body washing system based on this effect, which is what he did. Much later it resulted in a prototype for the house he developed.

It can take years of trial and error for principles to reach the level of an existing application. Even then there is no guarantee that it will become 'big' in mass

4
'Everything I know' session 01, YouTube video (accessed 1 March 2016).

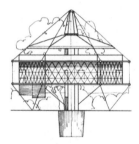

5

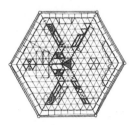

Buckminster Fuller, plan for Hexagonal 4D Dymaxion House, 1929. © Estate of R. Buckminster Fuller.

6
Polyphasic sleep, see Wikipedia.

markets. The first object that helped establish Buckminster Fuller's reputation was the unique proposition for his 4D house.[5] He had previous and unlucky experience in rather conventional prefab housing design with his father-in-law and their company Stockade. This new '4D House' was something else. It had a hexagonal floor plan, glass on all sides and the main aluminium structure was suspended from a central column, to favour tension forces and material reduction. The designer was allowed to display his design in a Marshall Field's department store in Chicago in 1929. The store hired copywriter Waldo Warren to come up with a less exclusive name for the house than '4D' After listening to Buckminster Fuller for two days he composed 'Dymaxion' out of the snippets DYnamic MAXimum and tensION. It was to become Buckminster Fuller's personal brand. He used it for many of his designs, for his aforementioned Chronofiles and also for the sleep schedule he followed, which consisted of four 30-minute naps per day,[6] excruciating to most people.

The first Dymaxion House was a scale model. It represented the crossroad of an unconventional invention and a department store's mission to present 'the future' as a mirage of desire and of course as an incentive to consume. Times were different. The future still held the promise of limitless satisfaction for everyone. The convenience that new products were expected to provide and that would virtually render man omnipotent, defined culture, particularly in the USA. The future ideal was in fact one of the driving forces behind streamline styling, the decorative copying of aerodynamic forms in everyday products, including even pencil sharpeners. Another magnificent example to illustrate yesterday's future-mindedness: in 1939 the World Fair was held in New York.[7] It featured a huge General Motors attraction called Futurama in which

7

Futurama at New York World Fair, designed by Norman Bell Geddes, 1939.

Ed van Hinte

thousands of visitors per day could experience the future as a scale model that they could overlook from moving chairs. After that they got to see some of the scale model cars in life size. To prove that they had gone through a time travel adventure they received a button at the exit that read: 'I have seen the future'.

Currently the future doesn't hold a strong position in the minds of designers and architects. Most of them are involved in reuse of what is already there. Their work would make more sense if they would also look for opportunities to develop principles for future reuse.

Prototypes

To Fuller the house was not just an attractive show-case of times to come. He was dead serious and had developed a range of different housing ideas based on his suspension principle. The most spectacular concept was a ten-floor tower that was to be light enough to be carried to the North Pole by the largest Zeppelin ever built. There a bomb would be dropped to create a crater in the ice for the building to stand in. Rather than an actual plan, this was the challenge that the designer put up for himself to make sure his design was indeed transportable and all-weatherproof and that it could be placed just about anywhere on Earth.

Richard Buckminster Fuller continued working on the house for many years. He wanted it to become a genuine mass product that would not be designed specifically for a site and would be functional and protective against all outside influences, including earthquakes. It was to be autonomous and independent.

In later versions the design became circular and extremely lightweight, with aluminium construction technology borrowed from the aircraft industry of the

Second World War. On top of the dome-shaped roof was a streamlined ventilator that turned with the wind and took care of inside climate control, with the help of especially designed division of spaces. Buckminster Fuller used a system that he had seen working quite well in grain silos. The natural airflow did not require extra climate adjustments, so inhabitants did not need to open the acrylic windows, which saved mechanisms, insulation and weight. The design was such that one person could put the house together. No part was heavier than five kilograms.

This redesign was built to be tested in prototypes. It included a grey water based toilet system to reduce water consumption and instead of a shower a 'fogger' was installed: here we have the principle Fuller discovered as a young navy engineer. It worked with compressed air and small water particles to provide a comfortable feeling. Floor surface was settled at about 90 square meters, average for an American family just after the War. The weight however was admirably low at just under 3 tons, just a fraction of the 150 tons that were considered normal.

Two Dymaxion House prototypes were combined in a two-story house, which was named the Wichita house.[8] It was built in Wichita, Kansas by real estate investor William Graham who acquired the prototypes from Fuller Houses Inc. after a lawsuit. The firm collapsed because, despite the promising market, Buckminster Fuller refused to sell houses before they were fully developed. He was a perfectionist. With hindsight he was probably right. It is risky to start a business with unconventional products. Unexpected faults may turn up, with dire consequences. Innovations need time and experience to mature.

8

Wichita House: a Combination of two prototypes of the Dymaxion Dwelling Machine designed by Buckminster Fuller, c. 1948. © Estate of R. Buckminster Fuller.

Lightweight

Another design that survived as a promising and unusual idea was the Dymaxion Car. Buckminster Fuller and his team built it with an engine and a rear axle that he obtained from Ford. At first, in 1928, it was going to be a flying car with inflatable wings. As the process went on the wings disappeared and the idea mutated into a car with a tail that would be lifted by the air at cruise speed. Eventually the tail was to remain on the ground.[9] Unfortunately, a floating tail doesn't contribute to stability and with such an unusual design in mind it is safer to start from a road vehicle and see what the concept may lead to.

9

Second prototype of the Dymaxion Car designed by Buckminster Fuller, 1934. © Estate of R. Buckminster Fuller.

The triangular aerodynamic car that Fuller finished in 1933 had remarkable qualities. Although made with some standard Ford parts it weighed only about five hundred kilos, half as much as the car for which the engine was designed and even very light by today's standards. It could carry eleven people, whereas the Ford could manage only four. The Dymaxion three-wheeler burnt half the amount of fuel the Ford needed. It still looked a bit like a wingless plane and a video shows that, because of its rear wheel steering, it had a very small turning circle.[5] It also must have been quite fast on straight roads, with a maximum speed of over 200 km/h.

Unfortunately, one of the three prototypes crashed, killing the driver, which doesn't help if your design is so different from the usual. It was a two-car accident and the driver of the other car, a politician, was responsible, but his car was quickly removed from the scene. The media didn't know and blamed the freakiness of Fuller's vehicle. A second prototype survived in obscurity and was probably scrapped in the 1950s. Only one prototype survived and is now in the National Automobile

Museum in Reno, Nevada. Two replicas were built in later years: one commissioned by British architect Norman Foster, who worked with Fuller for twelve years, the other by the Lane Motor Museum in Nashville, Tennessee.

The reason that the Dymaxion project was axed is unclear, because car manufacturers did show interest, as happened with the house. Whereas Buckminster Fuller's perfectionist attitude may have been the reason of commercial failure for the Dymaxion House, the appearance of the Dymaxion Car was believed by some to jeopardize the car industry. Banks allegedly were afraid that the used car market would collapse and that conventional car sales would drop. They withdrew money from further development. On the other hand it is not certain whether the Dymaxion Car would have posed a real threat. Consumers abide by the conventional. Industrial design pioneer Raymond Loewy had a name for this principle: MAYA he called it: Most Advanced Yet Acceptable. The two best-known Dymaxion products may well have been too advanced for broad acceptance.

Spheres

10

A geodesic dome designed by Buckminster Fuller as the U.S. pavilion at Expo 67 Montreal, 1967. © Estate of R. Buckminster Fuller.

For the geodesic domes[10] that Fuller developed their state of unusualness was far less of a problem, since a dome, certainly a large one, is not a consumer product. It is perceived as a building and a rather abstract and inconspicuous type of building too. This may be the main reason why domes were Fuller's one true commercial success. Over 300,000 were built for a wide range of purposes and in different sizes. Some were built for events, others for people to live underneath, still others to protect radar facilities. The geodesic

Ed van Hinte

WE CAN MAKE
ALL OF HUMANITY
SUCCESSFUL
THROUGH
SCIENCE'S

WORLD-ENGULFING INDUSTRIAL EVOLUTION

principle to create large and extremely light structures is now well understood.

Buckminster Fuller was not the original inventor of the principle. Most inventions happened earlier than believed. Carl Zeiss's chief engineer Walther Bauersfeld designed the first geodesic dome just after the First World War for his telescope installation. And geodesic airframes devised by Barnes Wallis were operational in Vickers warplanes in the 1930s. Fuller recognized the full potential of geodesic designs. He was the one who turned the invention into something quite spectacular and familiar. Buckminster Fuller:

> When I invented and developed my first clear-span, all-weather geodesic dome, the two largest domes in the world were both in Rome and were each 150 feet in diameter. They are St. Peter's, built around A.D. 1500, and the Pantheon built around A.D. 1. Each weighs approximately thirty thousand tons. In contrast, my first 150-foot-diameter geodesic all-weather dome installed in Hawaii weighs only thirty tons—one-thousandth the weight of its masonry counterpart. An earthquake will tumble both the Roman 150-footers, but would leave the geodesic unharmed.[11]

[11] www.synchronofile.com.

The bottom circle of a dome has to withstand the weight of everything above it. In the structural sense the main function of a dome therefore is to carry its own weight. Because of this a lightweight dome doesn't have to suffer as much from gravity as a heavy one does. That is the first reason of the success of geodesic domes.

The second is what is known as 'structural integrity'. A classic dome consists of layers of stones stacked on top of each other. Gravity holds them together, aided by cement or concrete. Other forces than gravity, such as the ones caused by an earthquake, may cause the whole thing to collapse. A geodesic dome on the other hand is capable of dealing with other forces, because it functions as one whole object. If one tries to lift a classic dome by the top, it breaks off. A geodesic dome, however, will not come apart. It holds its sturdiness within itself, like a football.

The word geodesic defines a 'straight' line on a curved surface. It was originally used to measure the planet we live on. A geodesic dome is designed along such curved lines, which are materialized as a lattice of, for instance, metal pipes, or plates with folded edges. The geodesic lines intersect to form triangles and a triangle is just about the most rigid structure we know. The triangle keeps fences and houses and skyscrapers up, because each corner has no place to go without the two others. Once the principle was established, the design of a dome became relatively simple. Generally it starts from a twenty-sided form of which each equilateral (but curved) triangle is subdivided into smaller triangles. Scale, materials and function determine the design. Domes have been applied in many different ways to perform many different tasks: radar stations, storage spaces, and auditoriums. The 1964 World Fair featured a dome as a pavilion designed by Thomas C. Howard. After redesign it became an aviary for the Flushing Meadows Queens Zoo.

Earth

The largest dome so far is the Fukuoka Dome in Japan (built in 1993), measuring 216 meters in diameter. It covers a baseball stadium. Buckminster Fuller, togeth-

Ed van Hinte

er with architect Dhoji Sadao, made a plan for an extremely large three-kilometre wide dome over midtown Manhattan in 1960. It didn't happen. The idea of a bright future in a controlled environment is more symbolic than real. There is no experience with controlling the climate in such a large structure. It may leak water from the outside and if it doesn't, irrigation will be needed for vegetation inside. And what happens when there is a fire?[12] Cities haven't been domed so far. Occasionally new plans arrive, such as the one to enclose the centre of Houston, Texas in 2010. Dubai has presented plans in 2014 to build a four square kilometre dome to cover a shopping area. Climate control inside a dome-shaped greenhouse in such an extremely hot area is expected to come at considerable environmental costs. Large domes give rise to doubt. They may keep the weather outside, but they may also enclose problems of various kinds. In brief: the costs are doubtful and the benefits unclear.

It is safer to think big on a more modest scale. A good example is Buckminster Fuller's development of a projection method to map the world. On a small globe areas, countries, regions are pictured roughly as they are, with the same proportions. Maps in an atlas are flat projections of curved surfaces, created perpendicular to Earth's rotational axis. As a consequence they come with considerable deformations, particularly in polar regions. Canada and Siberia are not as formidable as they look in conventional atlases. He figured out a globe with equally distributed projections on flat surfaces, thereby minimizing deformation. It could be printed on paper and consequently folded to become a tetrakaidecahedron, an equally divided fourteen-sided form.[13] This happens to be the shape of a soap bubble enclosed on all sides by other soap bubbles. Since Fuller's approach was purely geometric, it is uncertain if he was aware of this.

12
www.quora.com/Can-a-geodesic-dome-over-a-city-work-in-practicality.

13

Buckminster Fuller, Dymaxion Map, 1946.

14

R. Buckminster Fuller,
*Operating Manual for
Spaceship Earth*
(Carbondale: Southern
Illinois University Press,
1968). Available as pdf at
www.designsciencelab.com.

15
R. Buckminster Fuller,
see Wikipedia.

16
Claude Lichtenstein and
Joachim Krausse,
*Your Private Sky: R.
Buckminster Fuller. The
Art of Design Science*
(Zürich: Lars Müller
Publishers, 1999).

17
Club of Rome, see
Wikipedia.

18

Donella H. Meadows et
al., *The Limits to Growth:
a Report for the Club of
Rome's Project on the
Predicament of Man-
kind* (New York: Universe
Books, 1972).

Buckminster Fuller also chose a modest angle when he designed the geoscope, a transparent geodesic sphere with images of the continents on the inside so you could observe the position of Earth in relation to the stars from there. He saw us from far away, and contributed to popularization of the notion that humanity has to share this small planet, travelling at enormous speed through the Universe. In his book *Operating Manual for Spaceship Earth* (1968),[14] he demonstrated that he recognized the limitations of humanity living together on a ball with limited resources. The following quotation of his reflects his approach to fossil fuels:

> ...we can make all of humanity successful through science's world-engulfing industrial evolution provided that we are not so foolish as to continue to exhaust in a split second of astronomical history the orderly energy savings of billions of years' energy conservation aboard our Spaceship Earth. These energy savings have been put into our Spaceship's life-regeneration-guaranteeing bank account for use only in self-starter functions.[15]

This text subtly indicates that he saw the potential of humanity saving the world. He didn't agree with the Club of Rome, because in 1973 he found its approach too Malthusian.[16] The Club of Rome is a global think tank on political and environmental issues.[17] In 1972 it published its first report *The Limits to Growth*,[18] which had quite an impact at the time, because on the basis of increasing consumption it predicted the end of the world's resources within the foreseeable future. Malthus was a British preacher and demographer from the eighteenth century who also believed that population growth was increasing so quickly that food production

Ed van Hinte

would fall short in the near future. So far Mr. Malthus has been proven wrong, due to continuous improvement of food production. In fact the relative number of people suffering from insufficient nutrition is decreasing despite the growth of the world population.

In *The New Yorker* magazine (June 9, 2008) journalist Elisabeth Kolbert posed a very good question about Fuller, concerning an exhibition about his work at the Whitney Museum of American Art: 'Was he an important cultural figure because he produced inventions of practical value or because he didn't?' Buckminster Fuller certainly was an inspiring figure. He stimulated designers and architects to reflect on the future and pointed the way to create a better life for more people with minimum consumption of resources.

Technology and design have evolved and attention for social issues has increased, but the main dynamic principle 'do more with less' remains. Fuller had a typical engineering approach, trying to liberate mankind from effort. We will never know if the world would have been a better place if the Dymaxion House and Vehicle would have been commercially successful. His mission, however, is still proving its quality, particularly because he was not concerned with fighting the side effects of technology and mass consumption, but rather with spreading knowledge using technology itself to render Earth liveable in the future.

The Nobel Prize winning 'Bucky Ball', a symmetric carbon molecule first created by Harold Kroto, Sean O'Brien, Robert Curl, and Richard Smalley, now is a micro-monument for a man who devoted himself to nothing smaller than the sustainability of human life through application of physical principles. Richard Buckminster Fuller never knew about this molecule that was named after him, but his dome designs contributed to its definition. He still stimulates us to keep on learning.

The Humanitarian Object
Victor Papanek and the Struggle for Responsible Design

Alison J. Clarke

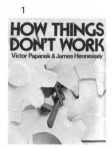

1

Victor Papanek, James Hennessey, *How Things Don't Work* (New York: Pantheon Books, 1977).

2

Interview with K. DeWitt, 'Gadgets That Don't Work Bother Designer', *The Victoria Advocate* 30 June 1977.

In 1977, a radical new book titled *How Things Don't Work*[1] hit the shelves in the US. With chapter titles including 'Share Your Lawn Mower Lady?', 'How Your Bathtub Doesn't Work' and 'No Roast Tonight—the Lights on My Carving Knife Need Realignment', the publication was clearly intended as a humorous but provocative call to action aimed at a nation complacent to the whims and excesses of a fully-fledged consumer culture. Its authors, the designers Victor Papanek and James Hennessey, were established critics and educators of the ills of design 'gone bad'; a kind of design set on perpetuating product obsolescence rather than solving practical or social problems just as Vance Packard had warned of in his 1960 classic *The Waste Makers*. Despite its critical tone, *How Things Don't Work* differed because it also attempted to explain to a broader consumer public how and why certain designs were better, or more responsible, than others: 'I wanted a book that would put some decisions back in the power of ordinary people', Papanek declared.[2] US political rhetoric since the Second World War had relied upon the notion of an elevated standard of living, epitomized by the so-called 'kitchen debate', which saw Nixon and Khrushchev pitting the 'the American Way of Life' against the Soviet communist economy through the symbolism of worker's homes, and their contents, at the American National Exhibition, Moscow, 1959. Buoyed by the counterculture movements of the 1960s and the energy crisis of the 1970s, a growing disquiet regarding the disenfranchised, the unemployed, the non-affluent, and their exclusion of a product-filled 'high' standard of living began to emerge.

Papanek and Hennessey's book was a rallying call to designers and consumers alike to critically question the value of the stuff that surrounded their everyday lives—a 'Battle Against Cosmetic Styling'. As Ulli

Alison J. Clarke

Diemer put it in his 1978 book review,

> [A] couple of professional designers have taken a whole new look at this 'standard of living', in a book called *How Things Don't Work*. In it, they examine some of the possessions, which are supposed to add up to our high standard of living. Their message is that a lot of the appliances, tools, and devices of which we're so proud very often are badly designed, prone to break down, and don't satisfactorily do the job they are supposed to do. In short, they don't really work.[3]

Recognizing the originality of their argument, Diemer continued,

> ... they don't just stop at the details of design. They question the whole set-up that produces inefficient and foolish contraptions so that someone can make a profit, and they make very practical, but radical, suggestions about how to do things differently.[4]

The desire to generate new responsible and humanitarian objects was part of broader theoretical shifts of the late 1960s and 1970s within political ecology and anthropology. Both disciplines had seen the mass destruction of environments and indigenous communities. A culture of commodity critique and what might loosely be described as an 'anti-design' movement came to the fore, in which the very nature of the material object was debated, its meanings and values brought into question. The neo-Marxist theorist Wolfgang Haug published *Kritik der Warenästhetik* (1971) critiquing the role of design (and advertising) in transforming bare-

3
Review by Ulli Diemer, 'How Things Don't Work: Victor Papanek & James Hennessey', *Seven News* August 1978.

4
Ibid.

faced commodities into desirable and delusionary entities, a system of enchantment which made 'people conditioned to enjoy what betrays them'. As the key driver of exchange-value, Haug expanded the Frankfurt School critique of popular culture and consumer objects as the symptoms of 'false consciousness', by focusing on the agent of manipulation—namely design—rather than the forms of commodities. The rise of radical ecology, feminist analysis, phenomenological theories, and the popularization of anthropological discourse saw the emergence of a critical design culture that sought to unpick the layers of 'false' meaning around commercial products. In this process, crafted, indigenous and artisanal objects laid claim to a type of authenticity that mass-produced, industrial objects did not possess. The shift towards the theories of phenomenology, away from the familiar dualisms of structuralism coupled with a newly theorized economic anthropology, generated alternative 'non-capitalistic' understandings of design as a collective, creative practice: material culture as an embodied entity of vital social value that operated beyond formal aesthetics. Rather than considering design as a merely Western industrial phenomenon, these new approaches put equal emphasis on objects of folk and indigenous culture as examples of an alternative design ideology usurping the primacy of industrial production.

Haug's work was translated into English as *A Critique of Commodity Aesthetics: Appearance, Sexuality, and Advertising in Capitalist Society* in 1986,[5] timely when considering the rise of the 'star designer'-cult-propelled figures such as Philippe Starck to the position of demi-gods with the capacity to transform ordinary everyday items, such as a lemon squeezer, into fetishes of a newly buoyant economy. The rise of the 'irresponsible object' of the 1980s is all the more

5

Wolfgang Fritz Haug, *Critique of Commodity Aesthetics: Appearance, Sexuality and Advertising in Capitalist Society* (Cambridge: Polity Press, 1986).

Alison J. Clarke

intriguing considering the unprecedented shift toward socially responsible design that had dominated the proceeding decade.

In 1970, Papanek's polemic *Design For the Real World: Human Ecology and Social Change*, a critique of advertising and ill-designed, mass-produced commodities cast him in the US tradition of consumer rights activists such as Ralph Nader. But Papanek, an Austrian émigré, asserted a distinctively European approach in his critiques that sat alongside those of fellow émigrés and contemporaries such as André Gorz, Ivan Illich and Bernard Rudofsky. He launched his design career combining a neo-Frankfurt School perspective with an ethnographic approach to the critique of consumer culture that fed on a broader ambivalence towards US popular culture. In a conversation with a journalist, Papanek traced his interest in socially responsible design back to the start of his design career in the 1950s. Working for a conventional design firm (he would later suggest during this period he worked with Raymond Loewy, the 'Father of Streamlining'), Papanek had a revelation regarding the ethnocentrism of industrial design. In an article entitled, 'Gadgets That Don't Work Bother Designer', Papanek recounted how he

> ... realized that while Americans are tall—this was before all the nutritional improvement in diet in Europe—most Europeans were not. Then there were Africans, Asians and South Americans. The rest of the world in fact that the design establishment was ignoring.[6]

6
Interview with K. DeWitt.

By the 1960s, working collectively with students and other members of faculty, Papanek began to devise a type of 'humanitarian object' that appealed to the likes of UNESCO rather than the good taste design institutions such as the Museum of Modern Art, which celebrated big name designers such as Charles Eames and George Nelson. Collaborating with student George Seeger on a prototype low-tech radio receiver unit for 'underdeveloped countries', he used a recycled juice can, transistor, earplug, wire, paraffin wax and wick.[7] The battery-less creation was engineered to allow indigenous users to top-up the design with cow dung as a sustainable power source. The idea was to distribute the item as an appropriate technology of mass communication amongst tribal groups and communities in 'pre-literate' parts of the world. Manufactured locally for less than 9 cents a unit, the design was supported by UNESCO as a model of participatory and co-design. In the twenty-first century, the project has come to stand for the broader ambitions of a late-postwar counterculture design geared towards social inclusion and pitted against corporatized power. Prototypes such as the tin-can radio represented a major change in design thinking, and highlighted the social potential of the designer working in co-design or user-based contexts. The design was included in Papanek's best-selling book, *Design for the Real World: Human Ecology and Social Change* (1970) supported by an anecdote regarding his clash with the elite members of High Modernism.

Once, visiting the Hochschule für Gestaltung at Ulm, in the 1960s, he gave a slide show of his humanitarian design, explaining how the tin-can radio could be decorated with indigenous ornament from applique to sequins and shell-work in keeping with the user-groups own decorative traditions. In Papanek's recollection, to 'allow' users to sully the purity of the industrial form, left the Ulm professors horrified. Disbelief and condemnation were followed by the suggestion to paint the tin-can a tasteful, industrial pale grey instead. 'But painting it would have been wrong', Papanek countered,

7

Victor Papanek and George Seeger, tin can radio receiver, early 1960s. © Victor J. Papanek Foundation, University of Applied Arts, Vienna.

Alison J. Clarke

BATTLE AGAINST

COSMETIC STYLING

'[f]or one thing, it would have raised the price of each unit by maybe one twentieth of a penny each.' Above all, however, he pointed out, 'I feel that I have no right to make aesthetic or "good taste" decisions that will affect millions of people in Indonesia, who are members of a different culture'.[8] Papanek contrasted this inclusive social responsible approach with the morally bankrupt nature of most Western industrial design, declaring

> When human wants do not exist, we invent them: 14-carat golf tees, mink-covered toilet seats, electric carving knives and electronic nail polish dryers are fostered and sold to an unsuspecting public who consent to this perversion of design and taste.[9]

In an article entitled 'Do-It-Yourself Murder', Papanek accused designers of generating dangerous goods that might even maim or kill. 'Members of the profession have lost integrity and responsibility and become purveyors of trivia', warned Papanek, continuing, '[yet] the health and energy requirements of the world's people ... lie well within the scope of long-range design planning'.[10]

Other socially responsible designs included an 'Off-Road Vehicle', devised with students at the North Carolina State University School of Design, inspired by the observation that '[o]ver two billion people stand in need of some of the most basic tools and implements'.[11] The vehicle was moulded from a 'fibregrass' 'using conventional chemical fibre-glass catalysts , but substituting dried native grasses ... for the expensive fibre glass mats'.[12] Intended for use in extreme terrain of undeveloped countries, it was ultimately discontinued due (according to Papanek) to ecological reasons. Openly condemning patents, seeing designs as open source, Papanek claimed that numerous companies had subsequently copied the idea.

8

Victor Papanek, *Design for the Real World: Human Ecology and Social Change* (New York: Pantheon Books, 1971), p. 164.

9
Victor Papanek, 'Pop Culture', *The Raleigh Times* 17 August 1963, p. 11.

10
Victor Papanek, 'Do-It-Yourself Murder: Social and Moral Responsibilities of Design', *SDO Journal* (1968), p. 26. See Alison J. Clarke, 'The Chrome-Plated Marshmallow: 1960s Consumer Revolution and its Discontents', in *You Say You Want a Revolution: Records and Rebels 1966–70* (London: V&A, 2016), p. 257

11
Papanek, *Design for the Real World*, p. 171.

12
Ibid., p. 173.

This type of 'humanitarian object' did not escape critique. On the rear cover of the 1971 edition of *Design for the Real World*, a former Finnish student of Papanek's offered an insight into the emerging politics around westerners designing for the 'underdeveloped':

> Today there is much controversy about design responsibility. And inevitably in discussions and articles Victor Papanek is mentioned. Some think he is too political, others think he is not political enough; some that he encourages neo-colonial exploitation, others that he is selling out the white race.[13]

13
Barbro Kulvik-Siltavuori, back cover text, Papanek, *Design for the Real World*.

14
Teresa Hayter, *Aid as Imperialism* (Harmondsworth: Penguin, 1971).

With publications such as *Aid as Imperialism* (1971) by Teresa Hayter,[14] the notion of the humanitarian object was increasingly open to scrutiny.

Nevertheless by 1979, published in over twenty languages, *Design for the Real World* had provided a generation of designers with an easily accessible insight into the so-called 'Design Needs for Developing Countries' discourse. It is clear that Papanek's ideas had impacted on conventional design institutions when, that year, Arthur J. Pulos, President of the International Council of Societies of Industrial Design (ICSID) gave an opening speech titled 'The Profession of Industrial Design' at the ICSID congress in Mexico City, October 14, 1979. 'In the century to come', declared Pulos,

> the design professions, with industrial design in the vanguard, will rededicate their efforts toward the final emancipation of all humans from drudgery and social and economic subjugation ... human beings in a new Renaissance will, once again, become the masters of their environment as the race achieves, finally, that ultimate form of equilibrium known as peace.[15]

15
See Alison J. Clarke, 'Design for Development, ICSID and UNIDO: The Anthropological Turn in 1970s Design', *Journal of Design History* 29, no. 1 (2016), pp. 43–57.

Alison J. Clarke

The Green Imperative

Following the international success of his ground-breaking and provocative debut book *Design for the Real World*, Papanek had co-produced several books by the time Pulos took his stand. *Nomadic Furniture* (1973) and *Nomadic Furniture II* (1974), followed by *How Things Don't Work* (1977), all co-authored with his life-time friend and former colleague James Hennessey. Papanek continued his critique of design aimed at superficial rather than real human needs in his sole-authored 1983 book *Design for Human Scale*, a polemical extension to *Design for the Real World*. His last book *The Green Imperative: Natural Design for the Real World* published in 1995, twenty-five years after the release of *Design for the Real World*, stood as a testament to the author's life-long commitment to socially responsible design.

The Green Imperative[16] represented Papanek's ultimate incorporation into the international design establishment. Research and writing for the book were supported by a US National Endowment for the Arts 'Distinguished Designer Award' as well as an 'Outstanding Design Award' from the IKEA Foundation, the Netherlands. As a tenured Professor of Design at the University of Kansas, his favourable circumstances stood in stark contrast to those surrounding the publication of the author's seminal first text, *Design for the Real World*, the critical tone of which had caused consternation within the USA design fraternity and saw Papanek ostracized by the mainstream design community. Support for the writing of *The Green Imperative* also revealed the changing emphasis within the design industry itself, which, in the decades since Papanek's first book, had finally acknowledged his prescience of environmental and social issues.

16

Victor Papanek, *The Green Imperative: Ecology and Ethics in Design and Architecture*, (London: Thames & Hudson, 1995).

Whether or not Papanek intended *The Green Imperative* as his final book is uncertain. But the work itself was clearly conceived as the culmination of his lifelong interest in the transformation of design from a practice of corporate profiteering to one of humanitarian significance. The acknowledgements towards the end of *The Green Imperative*'s introductory chapter, titled 'The Power of Design', act as homage to the significant companions of his career. Papanek was not known as a person to easily embrace any form of sentimentality, which suggests these heartfelt acknowledgements were penned by an elderly author aware that this might be the end of his life's work.

The shifting titles of the book, which gave an overview of design's relation to the natural world, the significance of objects embedded in everyday rituals, rather than the formalism of good taste aesthetics engineered by design corporations and museums, was revealing. The US edition of the book featured the subtitle 'Natural Design For the Real World' consciously drawing on the fame of Papanek's original best-selling book. Significantly, considering Papanek's repeated assertion that the European design world appreciated him more enthusiastically than the US (he had been ousted from the formal institutions of American industrial design in the 1960s), the UK edition utilized a more nuanced subtitle, 'Ecology and Ethics in Design and Architecture' revealing the gulf in the respective marketing perceptions.

A decade, therefore, appears to have lapsed between the writing of *Design for Human Scale*, and his final, *The Green Imperative*. However, during this period Papanek had in fact been working on an incomplete and unpublished manuscript titled 'The Edifice Complex: Thoughts on Architecture and Design in an Age of Greed'. Ostensibly based on his lifelong collection of teaching materials, lectures and articles formulated

Alison J. Clarke

during the period 1984 to 1989, the title was drawn from a 1986 acceptance speech he had delivered on receipt of an honorary doctorate at the University of Zagreb, awarded for 'humanising technology through industrial design'. Papanek's intention had been to include the more ephemeral aspects of his design journalistic work, along with his Zagreb University speech, to address the unabated, market-driven environmental destruction of the world's resources. However, 'The Edifice Complex' remained unpublished when, in 1991, the Thames & Hudson publisher began negotiations for the book that would become *The Green Imperative*.

By 1991, *The Green Imperative* had supplanted any of Papanek's other publication ambitions, but the work would draw heavily on previously published and pre-existing non-published works including the incorporation of two chapters from the unfinished 'Edifice Complex' manuscript. Strongly supported by the design editor at Thames & Hudson publishing house, the volume brought together a lifetime's work around design as a practice geared toward the making of 'humanitarian' objects. Although intended to attract a new audience, a younger generation of ecologically aware designers and advocates, Papanek's final book ultimately proved anachronistic.

When the book was finally released in 1995, it was reviewed by Ken Isaacs, an American architect and designer and contemporary of Papanek's who himself had been involved in counterculture design through the making of Do-It-Yourself furnishings and conceptual living structures. Isaacs, like Papanek, had shunned the hegemony of US consumer culture in favour of low-cost and inclusive designs. Despite sharing Papanek's antipathy toward consumer capitalism and middle-class mainstream American values, Isaacs had embraced new technologies early on in his career. He created for example the 'Knowledge Box' (1962) a total-immersion chamber constructed to challenge traditional ways of learning through a sensory visual and sound environment for the captive viewer, showing cultural and political images without a narrator. His stance, in contrast to that of Papanek's, had been to embrace modernity and its technologies in the struggle for utopia, rather than retreating for cover in craft, indigenous and anthropological objects. Appearing in the journal *Design Issues* (MIT) the review revealed the extent to which Papanek's ideas had fallen out of favour, even with the design activists with whom he had once shared a radical platform in the late 1960s and 70s. For Isaacs viewed Papanek's call for spiritual reflection and the adoption of indigenous models of 'the good life' (reflected in integrated design forms such as the Mongolian yurt, or the Inuit ice dwelling) as being woefully out of sync with the enormity of the task that designers in the late twentieth century needed to address:

> Doesn't the extremity of our situation call for genuine depth of thought and suggestion? Isn't there a more serious nomenclature than that of one of the early chapter heads, 'Designing for a Safer Future'?

17
Ken Isaacs, 'Review: The Green Imperative: Design for the Real World by Victor Papanek', *Design Issues* 13, no. 2 (1997), p, 79.

18
Ibid.

he asked.[17] Isaacs went on to describe Papanek's style of polemic as mere 'whistling in the cemetery', finding irony in asking 'people who have been eviscerated by the synthetic hedonism of marketing using the magic of television' to find 'spiritual life by meditating in the check-out lane with a Swatch (while wishing for a Rolex)?'[18] Furthermore Papanek's ideas failed to take into consideration the rise of 'non-objects', the relevance of interactive and software design which defined a new era. Concluding that his polemic was 'compla-

Alison J. Clarke

cent and timid', Isaacs's words consigned Papanek, in the final years of his life, to an era of activism firmly located in the past.

The Legacy

Design For the Real World, in many respects, marks a key moment in the historiography of design anthropology, in that it argued that *tangible sellable commodities* should *not* be the concern of design 'for a real world'. Design in industrialized capitalist economies, unlike, for example, indigenous and socialist economies, stated Papanek, had been reduced to a non-critical practice generating evermore banal and unethical commodities.

The identification of the 'user' as an integral part of the design process is a key facet of late 1960s design activism, and one that would develop into key design corporation innovation policies. So, too, was a fascination with anthropology and ethnography. Papanek embraced anthropology, in the form of the humanitarian object, as a means of thinking about the social potentialities of design beyond the capitalist and industrialized paradigm.

The regard of localized, ethnographically anchored renditions of meaning that emerged through the approaches advocated by Papanek and his contemporaries has spread from the highly theorized realm of academia to the R&D departments of design companies keen to understand ever more diverse markets, social relations, and users. The transition from analogue to digital consumption, the deepening of the resource crisis, the blurring of product and service sectors, the development of new understandings of innovation and creativity, all bolstered by academic theories challenging a binary opposition between people and things, has then led to the formulation of an area loosely described as 'design anthropology', a field that at its best endeavours to find the humanity in design.

Alison J. Clarke

Counterculture and Anti-Design
Postmodern Appropriations of Utopia

Marjanne van Helvert

In the beginning of the second half of the twentieth century, socially committed designers in the western, industrialized world largely found themselves in a countercultural position. Consumer capitalist ideals and practices had come to dominate the design discipline, and mass production had democratized design culture to unprecedented levels in the industrialized countries, yet the 1960s and 1970s are also known for a number of critical designers and movements that posed alternatives to this status quo. Richard Buckminster Fuller's work influenced many, among them Stewart Brand, whose DIY-bible the *Whole Earth Catalog* of 1968 helped American hippies and dissidents build their self-supported, ecological communities. Meanwhile in Europe, an anti-modernist tendency inspired groups such as Superstudio and Archizoom to conceptualize radical urban utopias as a form of critique on the political detachment they perceived in the commercialization of architecture and design. In search of alternative ways of living and of designing, the 1960s and 1970s were a time of experiments outside the mainstream, as well as a foundational era for future attitudes within consumer capitalist society, as subcultures were quickly found to be fertile ground for profitable marketing strategies. It was a transitional time both in western design and society. It represents the last big wave of socially committed design before the new millennium, and a rupture between the Modernist past and the postmodernist future within the canon of western design history.

Industrial design was still dominated by functionalism and the International Style, which had its roots in high Modernism and produced some of the most famous design icons of the twentieth century.[1] The high times of the International Style had come when former Bauhaus members, such as Walter Gropius, Marcel

1
See for example the furniture designs by Charles and Ray Eames, Alvar Aalto, Charlotte Perriand, Florence Knoll, George Nelson, et cetera.

Marjanne van Helvert

Breuer, Ludwig Mies van der Rohe, and Herbert Bayer, had fled Nazi-Germany and settled in the United States in the 1930s. Especially in the post-war years, they latched on to the corporate world, which proved a sizable clientele. The Bauhaus ideals of democratizing and industrializing what they considered good design found an alternative gateway to proliferation within North American corporations and institutions. Their Modernist, functionalist aesthetics came to dominate architecture and design for much of the century, and Modernism's radical claims to universality still echo loudly within today's design culture. Even though they soon came under fire with the advent of postmodernism and postcolonial theory, Modernist design has become a widely accepted standard worldwide.

Whole Earth and DIY

Some of the most iconic images of 1960s counterculture are pictures of Drop City,[2] an artist and hippie community in rural Colorado, USA. Built from 1965 and already abandoned by the early seventies, it consisted of a small group of buildings inspired by Richard Buckminster Fuller's geodesic domes. The colourful, futuristic looking domes were made of metal car rooftops and other recycled materials, and after a flurry of media attention, many hippie communes sprang up following its example. The dome-based architecture of these communities was an attempt to put one of Buckminster Fuller's light construction principles into practice, and for the hippies it was a way to distinguish their self-built dwellings from conventional housing. They soon experienced that it was not the ideal prototype for a house after all, as the domes tended to leak, and were quite unpractical to furnish. Lloyd Kahn, who

2

Drop City, Trinidad, Colorado, c. 1968, Photo by Gilles Mahé. Collection Centre Georges Pompidou, MnamCCI, Kandinsky Library.

3
Lloyd Kahn, *Domebook 1*
and *2* (Los Gatos: Pacific
Domes, 1970 and 1971).

wrote two popular books on dome building in the early
seventies,[3] lived in one for a year before he decided
it was a failure and stopped reprinting his books. In a
2010 interview he recalls:

> I was looking at farm buildings along the side of
> the road and I remember thinking, 'God those
> are so simple. They're rectangular and the roof
> is just one plane, while we have a building with
> 105 different surfaces.[4]

4
Lloyd Kahn, 'Domogra-
phy'. Interview by Julianne
Gola and Yukiko Bowman,
Volume 24, (2010), p. 77.

Recognizing the do-it-yourself (DIY) ethic that the
counterculture communities put into practice, American entrepreneur Stewart Brand published the *Whole
Earth Catalog* in 1968. Subtitled 'Access to Tools', it was
a comprehensive product guide for anyone looking to
become self-sufficient. It featured reviews of products
such as tools, machines, clothing, materials, and books,
because information was also considered a tool, and it
listed prices and addresses of vendors where the products could be ordered. The Catalog became extremely
popular and influential in the US, especially within the
counterculture movement. It professed its anti-establishment attitude in stating as its purpose:

> We are as gods and might as well get used to it.
> So far, remotely done power and glory—as via
> government, big business, formal education,
> church—has succeeded to the point where
> gross defects obscure actual gains. In response
> to this dilemma and to these gains a realm of
> intimate, personal power is developing—power
> of the individual to conduct his own education,
> find his own inspiration, shape his own environ-
> ment, and share his adventure with whoever
> is interested. Tools that aid this process are

Marjanne van Helvert

DESIGN FOR PEOPLE'S NEEDS

RATHER

THEIR

RATHER

THAN

WANTS

sought and promoted by the WHOLE EARTH CATALOG.[5]

5
Stewart Brand, ed., *Whole Earth Catalog: Access to Tools* (Menlo Park, CA: Portola Institute, 1968).

This statement echoes libertarian sentiments voiced earlier by Brand's great inspirator Buckminster Fuller, who believed that politicians are unable to solve complex problems, but that designers and engineers are able to do so instead.[6] Brand expanded this view to include anyone who was willing to educate themselves independently. Despite the anti-capitalist ideas often associated with the counterculture movement, Brand had a more entrepreneurial, anti-establishment motivation and was focused on the use of technology as a tool for change. Today he promotes a vision of the future he calls ecopragmatism, which implies doing what is necessary at the moment, in which he includes controversial technologies such as nuclear power and bioengineering.[7]

6
See for example: Richard Buckminster Fuller, 'The Designers and the Politicians', in *Beyond Left and Right: Radical Thought for Our Times*, ed. Richard Kostelanetz (New York: William Morrow and Co. Inc., 1968), pp. 364–70.

7
Stewart Brand, *Whole Earth Discipline: An Ecopragmatist Manifesto* (New York: Viking, 2009).

The rural communes were part of a larger movement of people leaving the North American cities in an attempt to provide for themselves in the countryside. This exodus is referred to as a back-to-the-land movement, one of several such agrarian movements in history, which occur for example in times of crisis and food shortages, or as a reaction to the perceived ill effects of industrialization and urbanization. Many people in the 1960s and 70s in the western world declared cities unhealthy and uninspiring, and wanted to get away from the demands of consumerism and nine-to-five jobs, to go back to growing their own food and building their own houses. This back-to-the-land and hippie movement chimed in with the emergence of the environmental movement, which accounts for the long-standing identification of environmentalism with the political left. One of the main catalysts for the rise in environmental awareness at that time was *Silent Spring*,[8] a book by

8
Rachel Carson, *Silent Spring* (Boston: Houghton Mifflin, 1962).

American biologist Rachel Carson, published in 1962, which researched the effects of pesticides and other chemicals on the environment and on human health. It generated a wide debate, which eventually led to the instalment of several significant acts of environmental protection legislation in the United States and many other countries. Environmental awareness was important in most of the hippie and artist communes and other newly established rural communities, which often practised organic farming and ecological living and building using natural and recycled materials.

The term ecology became widely used at that time in science and in popular culture. In science it concerns itself with the interconnectedness of organisms, humans among them, and their environments, but it also came to be used in a more mystical, holistic sense of living together with nature. Its significance was well illustrated by the picture on the cover of the first *Whole Earth Catalog*. It had been Brand's personal mission to persuade NASA to release it for public use. It was one of the first photographs of our planet, of the 'whole earth', taken by a spy satellite that was far enough from the earth to view it in its entirety, floating in empty, black space. In the months before, Steward had petitioned with NASA to release the images, as he thought an image of the earth as a singular, isolated, and unified world would have a great impact on people, and could be instrumental in raising environmental awareness.[9]

Several designers answered to the popularity of DIY counterculture and the search for environmentally friendly alternatives with self-built furniture guides. Victor Papanek and James Hennessey published *Nomadic Furniture* in 1973,[10] which set out to show 'how to build and where to buy lightweight furniture that folds, inflates, knocks down, stacks, or is disposable and can be recycled', as it said on the cover. The au-

9
Robert Horvitz, 'Whole Earth Culture: Exploring Whole Earth', Whole Earth Catalog, wholeearth.com/history-whole-earth-culture.php (accessed 18 April 2016).

10

James Hennessey and Victor J. Papanek, *Nomadic Furniture* (New York: Pantheon Books, 1973).

Marjanne van Helvert

thors stated that it was meant for an ecologically responsible generation that is constantly on the move. In Italy, in 1974, designer Enzo Mari published *Autoprogettazione?* (Self-Design? or Self-Made?), a similar book with instructions for building simple furniture made out of wooden boards.[11] That same year, American designer Ken Isaacs came out with *How to Build Your Own Living Structures*,[12] a more experimental interpretation of ecological, modern living. The book introduced Isaacs's modular system for interior constructions based on different scales of cube structures to replace furniture, and ideas for micro-houses that promote spatial and material efficiency. A recent reincarnation of these projects is Hartz-IV Möbel[13] (German welfare furniture), an initiative by German designer Van Bo Le-Mentzel. Started as a blog and then also published in book form, Hartz-IV Möbel is ironically named after the German welfare system. The designer himself was on welfare when he decided to make a simple, affordable but well-designed chair, and put the instructions online for other people with a limited income. The chair was soon followed by other pieces of modernist-inspired furniture, all published for free on his website with detailed instructions and an overview of the material costs.

11

Enzo Mari, *Autoprogettazione?* (1974, reprint Mantova: Corraini, 2002).

12

Ken Isaacs, *How to Build Your Own Living Structures* (New York: Harmony Books, 1974).

13

Van Bo Le-Mentzel and Birgit S. Bauer, *Hartz IV Moebel.com: Build More— Buy Less: Konstruieren statt Konsumieren* (Ostfildern: Hatje Cantz, 2012).

Design for Need and Appropriate Technology

Besides the rise of environmental awareness, the influence of which in industrial design was then mostly still limited to the counterculture movements, the 1970s also saw the emergence of a socially responsible or humanitarian design in the western world. Designer Victor Papanek had argued not only for an environmental approach to design, but also for designers to assume responsibility in social issues. He urged them

14
Victor Papanek, *Design for the Real World: Human Ecology and Social Change* (London: Thames & Hudson, 2011), p. 219.

15
Ibid., pp. 234–47. For more on Papanek, see pp. 145-62 of this book.

'to design for people's needs rather than their wants',[14] which according to him especially meant focusing on 'the fields that design has neglected', among them design for the medical field, for the handicapped and the disabled, and design for the Third World.[15] In the western world industrial design and design education were increasingly thought to be an important part of development aid, as it was argued that they could be instrumental in the industrial development of 'Third World' countries. This idea culminated in a conference organized by the International Council of Societies of Industrial Design (ICSID) at the Royal College of Art in London in 1976. Its aim was to

> return to the earlier ideals of the profession of industrial design which aimed to meet the needs of the modern world by designing in human terms where social purpose combined with aesthetic expression and symbolic value.[16]

16
Julian Bicknell and Liz McQuiston, *Design for Need: The Social Contribution of Design: An Anthology of Papers Presented to the Symposium at the Royal College of Art, London, April, 1976* (Oxford: Published for ICSID by Pergamon Press, 1977), p. 7.

Aside from Papanek, German designer Gui Bonsiepe was one of the principal names associated with this movement. He was educated at the Hochschule für Gestaltung in Ulm – and later taught there – a short-lived but influential design school that can be seen as a post-war reincarnation of the Bauhaus, continuing its modernist ideas. After the closing of the HfG, he emigrated to South America, where he still lives and works, mostly on interactive and information design projects. In his contribution to the Design for Need conference Bonsiepe argued that 'what was needed was not design *for* developing countries but design *in* and *by* developing countries'.[17] This argument seems prescient of the criticism that the movement would receive, questioning the importing of western design to a culture or climate that it might not be suitable for. It has also been called a

17
Pauline Madge, 'Design, Ecology, Technology: A Historiographical Review', *Journal of Design History* 6, no. 3 (1993), p. 155, www.jstor.org/stable/1316005.

Marjanne van Helvert

neo-colonial or imperialist practice, as it relies on western designers working for developing countries, rather than focusing on vernacular design traditions and local people's expertise.[18] Some of the Design for Need discourse certainly sounds paternalistic, as evidenced by the following words of Misha Black, joint chairman of the organizing committee, which serve as a motto of the conference publication:

> We have two things to offer the emergent world: our technology—a power for good as well as evil—and the frail but real advantages of democracy. But if the rest of the world is to learn from us, we must prove ourselves worthy of the role of teacher.[19]

Some social design practices today are vulnerable to similar criticism, as they continue to rely on the assumption of the superiority of professional, western designers operating in a context that is foreign to them.[20]

Another concept that is associated with humanitarian design is appropriate technology, which finds its origins in *Small is Beautiful*, an influential book by economist E.F. Schumacher, published in 1973. The appropriate technology movement searched for small-scale, environmentally friendly solutions to problems, as an alternative to mainstream industrial design and technology that is aimed at mass production and perpetual growth. Examples of such functionalistic and cheap technologies can be seen in hand-powered machines, solar cookers, and self-built wind turbines. Although the concept of appropriate technology became very popular in the field of development aid, it was soon criticized for promoting inferior technologies to the poor and thus perpetuating inequality. Yet its influence can still be seen in many social design projects today.[21] Within the

18
For an overview of this critique see for example: Ann Brown, 'Neocolonialism in Design for Development', *Making Futures Journal* 3 (28 March 2014), www.plymouthart.ac.uk/documents/Brown_Ann.pdf.

19
Bicknell and McQuiston, *Design for Need*, p. 2.

20
For a case study and critique of contemporary social design projects see for example: Danah Abdulla, 'A Manifesto of Change or Design Imperialism? A Look at the Purpose of the Social Design Practice', in *A Matter of Design: Making Society through Science and Technology*, ed. Claudio Coletta et al. (Milan: STS Italia Publishing, 2014), pp. 245–60, www.stsitalia.org/conferences/STSITALIA_2014/STS_Italia_AMoD_Proceedings_2014.pdf.

21
A well-known example is the Hippo water roller, see: www.hipporoller.org. Another one is Little Sun, a solar-powered LED lamp developed by artist Olafur Eliasson and engineer Frederik Ottesen: www.littlesun.com.

current resurgence of environmentally friendly design, appropriate technology continues to be a strategy for sustainable solutions, and might be especially appropriate for promoting technology based on renewable power sources and other alternative solutions in the industrialized world.

Radical and Anti-Design

In Europe the proliferation of Modernist design and architecture was equally challenged by a new generation of designers, often grouped together as the Radical Design or Anti-Design movement. The Radical and Anti-Designers designed furniture as well, but are most famous for their architectural concepts. At the time, post-war Europe was being rebuilt according to Modernist urban planning principles inspired by Swiss architect Le Corbusier, which afforded the fast and efficient construction of much-needed residencies. High Modernism had seen its 'Utopian forms now degraded into anonymous forms of large-scale housing and office construction', as philosopher Fredric Jameson has aptly put it.[22] The Radical designers attempted to conceptualize the possible consequences of increased industrialization and urbanization for design and society, which took the form of utopian and dystopian architectural megastructures in their work. As these new urban visions were often difficult to reconcile with existing landscapes and infrastructures, most of the Radical design projects remained in a conceptual phase, often deliberately so, and were visualized and theorized in sketches, texts, photomontages, scale models, and performances. As a result, many of these concepts were communicated to the public through exhibitions rather than marketable objects, and acquired an intel-

22

Fredric Jameson, *Postmodernism, Or, The Cultural Logic of Late Capitalism* (Durham: Duke University Press, 1991), p. 314.

Marjanne van Helvert

lectual and sometimes mythological status through the years.

While their futuristic looking plans for ubiquitous urban landscapes and technological living structures show aesthetical and conceptual parallels, their ideological motivations and intentions varied widely. Some of these designers and groups of the late 1950s, the 1960s, and early 1970s were explicitly Marxist, while others celebrated capitalist consumer culture in their work. Some of them fervently rejected Modernism, yet others considered themselves the dutiful heirs of the 'primitives of modern architecture' and regarded their work as the next phase within the development of design.[23] What they had in common was a search for a revolutionary new type of city, one that would connect industrial design and technology to the demands of the free, modern citizen. They researched the connections between modern design and consumer capitalism, which were booming and transforming society, as they seemed very much aware of something that Fredric Jameson much later, in 1991, described in his seminal work *Postmodernism, or, The Cultural Logic of Late Capitalism*:

23
Superstudio, 'Superstudio: Projects and Thoughts', *Domus* 11 February 2012. www.domusweb.it/en/from-the-archive/2012/02/11/superstudio-projects-and-thoughts.html (accessed 29 April 2016). Originally published in *Domus* 479 (October 1969.)

> [A]esthetic production today has become integrated into commodity production generally: the frantic economic urgency of producing fresh waves of ever more novel-seeming goods (from clothing to airplanes), at ever greater rates of turnover, now assigns an increasingly structural function and position to aesthetic innovation and experimentation.[24]

24
Jameson, *Postmodernism*, p. 4.

Some Radical and Anti-Designers researched and exploited design's functioning as aesthetic innovation and in that sense they embody the end of the utopian

Modernist era, and the beginning of postmodernism.

In the late 1950s one of the forerunners of the super-architecture projects, Dutch CoBrA artist Constant Nieuwenhuys, started his utopian project New Babylon, a proposal for an endless, interconnected global city. For almost twenty years, initially while he was part of the Situationist International movement, Constant worked on scale-models, collages, and drawings that offered glimpses of what life in this ever growing, hypothetical, nomadic city-world would look like. He argued that increased technological production and automation would afford more people more leisure time and un-precedented freedom and creativity, which would trans-form society into the 'Marxist kingdom' of New Babylon. About its realization he wrote:

> The building of New Babylon can only begin once the economy is exclusively aimed at the satisfaction of our needs, in the widest sense of the term. Only such an economy permits the complete automation of non-creative activities, and consequently the free development of cre-ativity.[25]

A similar type of free citizen was envisioned by Hungar-ian-born French architect Yona Friedman, who devel-oped his idea of the Ville Spatiale (Spatial City) from 1956 onwards.[26] It allowed for existing cities to remain, while new, labyrinthine superstructures would be built in a raised grid above them in order to save valuable space at the ground level. The intention of his accompanying concept of Mobile Architecture was that citizens would construct their own flexible living arrangements within the superstructure, according to their wishes. Next to his architectural designs Friedman produced manuals for self-reliance in building and urban planning.[27]

25
Constant Nieuwenhuys, 'New Babylon', isites. harvard.edu/fs/docs/icb. topic709752.files/WEEK 7/ CNieuwenhuis_New Baby-lon.pdf (accessed 30 April 2016).Written by Con-stant for the exhibition catalogue published by the Haags Gemeentemu-seum, The Hague, 1974.

26

Yona Friedman, photo-montage of a Ville Spatiale over the Seine in the heart of Paris, 1959. Collection of Centre Georges Pompidou.

27
For more on his work, see: www.yonafriedman.com (accessed 30 April 2016).

Marjanne van Helvert

Inspired by this megastructure architecture as well as by the work of Buckminster Fuller, the group Archigram formed in London in 1961. Its principal members were Peter Cook, David Green, Michael Webb, Warren Chalk, Ron Herron, and Dennis Crompton. Their projects focused on the implementation of technology and a celebration of consumerism and hedonism in concepts for futuristic urban structures. They became famous for their iconic images of pod-like modular architectural designs, such as the Walking Cities and Plug-In Cities.[28] In Florence a few years later, a group of architects and designers decided to name themselves Archizoom as a critical parody of Archigram.[29] Its members Andrea Branzi, Gilberto Corretti, Paolo Deganello, Massimo Morozzi, Lucia Bartolini, and Dario Bartolini wanted to subvert modern, consumer society by exploiting its own system, through themes of pop culture and mass consumption. They believed that this was the only way to challenge the partnership of capitalism and Modernist design, and to free the working class of the bourgeois hierarchy of taste as well as class divisions themselves. One of their projects was Dream Beds,[30] a range of 'kitsch furniture capable of destroying the good taste of middle-class homes, like new Trojan horses'.[31] As Branzi later wrote about Archizoom's intentions: 'The optimism of modernity was replaced by an enthusiastic desire for its flop.'[32] Since their endeavour to liberate design from the taboo of kitsch has been quite successful, especially so within consumer culture itself, their opposite intentions may seem hard to grasp for us now.

Archizoom was part of a range of critical, left-leaning Italian groups active at that time, such as UFO, Gruppo 9999, Gruppo Strum, and, perhaps the most famous one, Superstudio, founded in 1966 by Adolfo Natalini and Cristiano Toraldo di Francia. Superstudio's

28
An archive of Archigram's work can be found on archigram.westminster.ac.uk (accessed 30 April 2016).

Ron Herron, Archigram, Walking City, originally called Cities: Moving, 1964.

29
Pier Vittorio Aureli, *The Project of Autonomy: Politics and Architecture Within and Against Capitalism* (New York: Temple Hoyne Buell Center for the Study of American Architecture, 2008), p. 71.

30

Archizoom Associati, Naufragio Di Rose Dream Bed, 1967.

31
Andrea Branzi, *No-stop City: Archizoom Associati* (Orléans: HYX, 2006), p. 146.

32
Ibid.

33

Superstudio, Continuous
Monument, 1969.

34
Adolfo Natalini, quoted
in: Jonathan Glancey,
'Anti-Matter', *The Guardian* 31 March 2003 www.
theguardian.com/artand-
design/2003/mar/31/
architecture.artsfeatures
(accessed 4 May 2016).

35
'Superstudio', Wikipedia,
en.wikipedia.org/wiki/
Superstudio (accessed 30
April 2016).

36

best-known project is the Continuous Monument,[33]
an architectural concept of an endless, mysteriously
monolithic structure stretching across the landscape.
It was intended as a dystopian 'warning of the horrors
architecture had in store with its scientific methods
for perpetuating standard models worldwide'.[34] Much
quoted, Natalini stated at a lecture in 1971:

> If design is merely an inducement to consume,
> then we must reject design; if architecture is
> merely the codifying of bourgeois model of
> ownership and society, then we must reject
> architecture; if architecture and town planning
> is merely the formalization of present unjust
> social divisions, then we must reject town plan-
> ning and its cities ... until all design activities are
> aimed towards meeting primary needs. Until
> then, design must disappear. We can live with-
> out architecture.[35]

The formal elements and visual aesthetics of Archizoom, Superstudio and other groups in the critical
Italian movement have proven to be very influential in
later years, yet their political message appears to have
been left in the past. After the peak of Radical and
Anti-Design in the late sixties and early seventies, their
colourful use of plastics and foams, kitschy decora-
tions, pop culture, and surrealist imagery soon became
characteristic of the apolitical and more commercial
postmodern movement, in design perhaps most iconically represented by the Italian studio Memphis.[36]
Within postmodernism the radical new style paradoxically came to be part of the commercial system it had
intended to subvert.

Ettore Sottsass, Memphis,
Casablanca Sideboard,
1981.

Marjanne van Helvert

Postmodern Post-Utopia

The establishment of industrial design as an autonomous discipline, which had only begun to be taken seriously since the Second World War, had coincided with the institutionalization of Modernism in the International Style in much of the western world. Still, if the Modernist design culture of the first half of the twentieth century survives as an elemental model of industrial design today, it is not because the countermovements of the 1960s and 1970s have not tried to undermine and transform it. Some of the most ideologically outspoken designers made a name for themselves in the US and in Europe in this period, with either very pragmatic or purely hypothetical proposals for new, utopian futures. They came from a generation that felt it had to rebuild and change the world, and they proposed radical and experimental alternatives to mainstream design and society. Yet they seem to have generated the last big waves in socially committed and utopian design in the western world, followed by almost three decades in which apolitical, postmodern, and commercial design dominated the design discipline.

In retrospect, the Radical, Anti-Design, and Counterculture movements appear to have formed a transitional moment between modernism and postmodernism, an evolutionary rather than a revolutionary period that opened up the arena of industrial design to ambiguity, reuse and reinterpretation of previous styles and dogmas, and to a new, more dynamic relationship with consumer society. The emergence of postmodern design, in which irony and pastiche erased or redirected any possible political content, may be seen as a sign of a design culture having consolidated within consumer capitalist society, successfully absorbing countermovements and deviating styles along the way.

Interestingly, this apolitical cultural era in western industrial design seems to have partly come to an end with the multiple crises in global politics, climate, and economy at the start of the new millennium, and a revived environmental awareness has instigated a new movement of social and sustainable projects in design.

Marjanne van Helvert

DESTROYING THE GOOD TASTE OF MIDDLE-CLASS

HOMES, LIKE NEW TROJAN HORSES

Design History Interrupted
A Queer-Feminist Perspective

Ece Canlı

The gender-laden design agenda has seen intriguing novelties in recent years: smart menstrual cups that control women's menstruation cycles remotely, apps that provide touch-screen masturbation tutorials for female users, multinational clothing brands that herald gender-bending or unisex seasons, and doll corporations that introduce miscellaneous body types, skin tones and gender presentations in their new models. The change is noteworthy, and reasonable, considering today's increasing voices and visibility of post-feminists, queers and other marginalized persons. Before deeming this move affirmative, it is important to understand how these designed 'things' contribute to the broader discussion around gender, sexuality and identity both within and outside the design discipline. To attain that, it is crucial to analyse the issue in question, namely queer-feminist design theory and practice, from a historical and critical viewpoint. This is what I will seek to undertake in this essay.

I will also dare to claim that there cannot be such thing as queer-feminist design history, but one can seek to capture different moments of theoretical and practical endeavours shuttling between past, present, future, and eventually, utopia. This kind of narration echoes what feminist graphic designer and scholar Martha Scotford has already called 'messy history' as an alternative way of recounting design activities that are non-normative, personal and expressive. Scotford opposes this to 'neat history' which is conventional, mainstream, dominantly white-male-middle-class and privileged.[1] Sheila Levrant de Bretteville, a prominent feminist graphic designer and scholar, relates this messy and non-linear temporality to women's quilts and patchworks. De Bretteville considers these works as material assemblages of personal experiences and fragments of time-space, in contrast to the patriarchal

1
Martha Scotford, 'Toward an Expanded View of Women in Graphic Design', *Visible Language* 28, no. 4 (1994), p. 371.

Ece Canlı

rationale that scorns individualization and favours universal verification.[2] My personal interpretation of queer-feminist design history in this essay will be as fragmented as a patchwork, and akin to a collage that will merge history, theory and practice with criticism.[3]

I am aware that I will inherently omit many existing, ongoing or vanished scholarly works and design practices.[4] While one reason for this omission is that many works are being done worldwide that stay under the radar, another is intentional and therefore personal. As the answer to 'what makes design theory, practice and research feminist' might vary from person to person, for me, it is discourse, critical stance and political engagement. Even if this engagement emerges from a particular artefact tackling gender discrimination, it should end up targeting greater power structures. For instance, the effort of bringing the neglected works of woman designers and architects into view has surely been significant from the 1970s onwards. However, such monographic initiations have also been criticized for repeating the modernist historiography, mostly based on 'pioneers' and 'stars' who are already privileged to access special education and professional milieus.[5] Thus, the projects of visibility that mostly align designers together just because they belong to the same gender presentation will not be included here. The role of design in gender disparity is a complex phenomenon, so, instead of recounting 'design works done by women' or 'products from women designers',[6] I will touch upon those works that have a political discourse and dedication for unravelling the intrinsic alliance between design and gender construction.

2
Sheila Levrant de Bretteville, 'A Re-examination of Some Aspects of the Design Arts from the Perspective of a Woman Designer', *Arts in Society* 11, no. 1 (1974), p. 117.

3
My criticisms towards gender-related design activities in this essay do not intend to despise or underestimate any struggle performed by women as a disadvantaged group. On the contrary, I acknowledge their significance and respect their own circumstances, and therefore, I analyse them critically as a part of the feminist common cause that would go beyond the context of design activity.

4
For instance, I acknowledge non-disciplinary design practices such as graphic works, artefacts or public interventions made by activists and DIY projects by alleged 'amateurs'. Nevertheless, in this essay, I will only take into account the works within or on the margins of the design discipline, for the sake of focus and clarity.

5
For an extensive critique about it, see Carma Gorman, 'Reshaping and Rethinking: Recent Feminist Scholarship on Design and Designers', *Design Issues* 17, no. 4 (2001), pp. 72–88.

6
There have been numerous exhibitions, publications, catalogues and conferences to make women designers visible. For some of them, see Liz McQuiston, *Women in Design: A Contemporary View* (London and New York, 1988); *Women Designers in the USA, 1900–2000: Diversity and Difference*, ed. Pat Kirkham (New York: The Bard Graduate Center for Studies in the Decorative Arts, Design and Culture, 2002); and more recently *Pathmakers: Women in Art, Craft, and Design, Midcentury and Today Exhibition* (New York: National Museum of Women in the Arts, 2016).

No ideology, school of thought or political agenda emanates out of nowhere independently of social contexts and paradigms. Likewise, the design discipline was thoroughly swayed by women's rising voices and visible exertions in social realms blasted open by the second-wave feminist movement, in the 1960s. Following the legal achievements of suffragettes who fought for the rights of women before the law, the second-wave feminists expanded the issue of women's liberation to a great deal of varied but correlated struggles: systematic discrimination of women in the workplace, domestication, anti-abortion enforcements, marital discords, uneven division of labour in the household, domestic violence, sexism, misogyny, and so on. Their resilience incited numerous disciplines and most conspicuously art.[7] Feminist artists and their works, imbued with profound political agendas of women, not only stirred up significant debates around gender, but also demonstrated aesthetic-political ways of using art as a medium to tackle, resist, and counteract the man-made (art) world.

A glowing feminist discourse did not, however, permeate from the artistic realm to the field of design immediately. In the early 1970s, some prominent figures started blurring the boundaries between art, graphic design, urban design and architecture. For instance, Susana Torre, co-founder of *Heresies Journal*,[8] not only laid bare the miswritten histories of woman architects along with the feminist critiques towards the notions of body, space and built environments; she also practised architecture to re-construct a non-sexist and egalitarian society.[9] Sheila Levrant de Bretteville, another eminent figure from art and graphic design, brought these two kindred fields together even further and ap-

7
Mostly visual and plastic arts, performing arts and performance art, crafts and conceptual art.

8

Heresies: A Feminist Journal on Art and Politics was active between 1977–1992, like an oasis in the male-dominated art and design scene and a free zone for women's knowledge exchange among the blurred boundaries of art, architecture, design, prose and poetry. For the archive of the past issues: heresiesfilm-project.org/archive/#.

9
www.susanatorre.net/architecture-and-de-sign/the-individu-al-and-the-collective/the-house-of-meanings.

Ece Canlı

proached the image-making process as a feminist tool to thwart male supremacy.[10] One of her iconic works that have inspired many successor artists and designers was the poster she designed for the Women in Design Conference held in Los Angeles in 1975.[11] Overturning the perception of hardware under the sway of the male user, she used eyebolts as visual concretizations of the Venus symbol, the female sign. Eyebolts, aligned as in parading till the horizon and heading towards an unknown but awaited future, symbolized the prospective visions of woman designers to be discussed during the conference. She also converted the eyebolt figures into necklaces that were distributed among the artists and designers at the conference and this became the symbol of the women's struggles and empowerment in design. This work was historically and politically significant in the sense that a designed image of an artefact (graphic of original eyebolt),[12] which was turned into another designed artefact (eyebolt shaped chained-necklace), demonstrated how material modification of one single figure would challenge and provoke a malestream[13] discipline while encouraging woman designers to act in solidarity.

Except the few above examples, it was not until the 1980s that design, as a disciplinary activity, was charged with a critical discourse and feminist stance. When it started, feminist designers from near and afar, with numerous agendas, attacked the existing status quo. Early feminist design scholars transformed Linda Nochlin's well-echoed question into 'Why have there been no great women designers?'[14] to confront long-standing male dominance and patriarchal hegemony in design history, applied practice and design academia. They outlined how women designers were either displaced from design practice and scholarship or overshadowed by their husbands, male work-partners

10
She was also co-founder of the experimental art and design space for women The Women's Building in California, opened in 1973, and the founder of The Feminist Workshop and Women's Graphic Center in it.

11

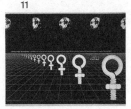

Sheila Levrant de Bretteville, poster for Women In Design Conference, 1975.

12

Sheila Levrant de Bretteville, Eyebolt necklace, 1972.

13
A mixture of 'male' and 'mainstream', mostly used in feminist parlance.

14
Linda Nochlin, 'Why Have There Been No Great Women Artists?', *Art News* 69, no. 9 (January 1971), pp. 22–39, 67–71.

15

Scotford 1994 (see note 2); and Cheryl Buckley, 'Made in Patriarchy: Toward a Feminist Analysis of Women and Design', *Design Issues* 3, no. 2 (1986), pp. 3–14.

16

'We live in a world designed by men; it's not for nothing that the expression 'man-made' refers to a vast range of objects that have been fashioned from physical material.' Philippa Goodall, 'Design and Gender', *block* 9 (1983), p. 50.

17

Judith Attfield, 'FORM/female FOLLOWS FUNCTION/male: Feminist Critiques of Design', in *Design History and the History of Design*, ed. John A. Walker, pp. 199–21 (London: Pluto Press, 1989); and Buckley, 'Made in Patriarchy'.

18

Pat Kirkham, ed., *The Gendered Object* (Manchester: Manchester University Press, 1996).

19

And this ideology presented itself 'neutral and ideology-free', Buckley, 'Made in Patriarchy', p. 11.

20

It is not a simple commonplace 'sex sells', but a systematic, organized process of objectification of the female body for the male gaze. For a scrutinized argument, see Judith Williamson, *Decoding Advertisements* (New York: Boyars, 1984), which bares an analysis of advertisements as the main transmitters of

or family members.[15] Moreover, some of them put dominant 'man-made'[16] design production in question and revealed how the discipline and its instruments reproduced the inferiority of 'FORM/female' to 'FUNCTION/male'. Because 'male' was associated with science, technology, machinery, public space, strength, assertiveness, rationality; 'female' with ornament, decoration, surface, domestic areas, fragility, spontaneity and emotion.[17] Such stereotypes were reflected not only in the contempt for the creative works (i.e. textile, jewellery, crafts, ceramics, decorative arts) practised by women as a result of their socio-political and economic status but also in the daily 'gendered objects'[18] and environments that systematically segregated bodies according to genders and sexes.

Besides, other scholars, similarly challenging design as a 'product of bourgeois, patriarchal ideology',[19] focused on the women's representation in consumer culture either as sexually objectified presenters used for marketing strategies[20] or passive domestic consumers. For instance, feminist critiques traced how, especially during the post-Second World War and Cold War era, women were targeted as potential consumers for capitalism-driven societies, and how the market, and thereby designed artefacts in it, went through 'feminization' to sell better.[21] They demonstrated the reciprocity between how technological artefacts and their marketing process were defined by gender codes, yet how gender codes were reproduced through the everyday objects.[22] Moreover, most of the products promoted as 'design for women' such as electrical appliances (i.e. microwaves, blenders, vacuum cleaners) did not

20 (cont.)

design ideologies. A previous leading source also can be seen: Erving Goffman, *Gender Advertisements* (New York: Harper & Row, 1976).

21

Penny Sparke, *As Long as It's Pink: The Sexual Politics of Taste* (London: Pandora and San Francisco: HarperCollins, 1995); Victoria de Grazia and Ellen Furlough, eds., *The Sex of Things: Gender and Consumption in Historical Perspective* (Berkeley: University of California Press, 1996).

22

Cynthia Cockburn and Susan Ormrod, *Gender and Technology in the Making* (London and Thousand Oaks: Sage, 1993).

Ece Canlı

lessen the women's workloads as alleged. On the contrary, they trapped women with a greater variety of work—with their 'saved time', thanks to technology—and underpinned their domestication as day labourers.

This paradigm shift, as one of the pieces in my patchwork, which I would like to call 'feminist-turn in design', constituted the backbone of the feminist discourse in design. This turn was an important endeavour that aimed to shake design to its patriarchal foundations by debunking its oppressive disposition and unfolded how 'man-made' things were the first-hand agencies in reproducing gender roles and corroborating power structures. Also, they have been an important inspiration for the newcomers to the field. However, if we lift our head from the linear feminist design pathway and see the time-space axis from a multidimensional perspective, we can also diagnose many shortcomings in these projects, which have yet to be overcome. With a critical stance, I would like to mention the most salient failures of their success.

A Critical Aperture in Criticality

First of all, scholarly critiques and theorizations have fallen short of practical implementations of what has been promised. How many design practitioners and initiators do we know since the 1980s who have genuinely worked on deconstructing existing gender segregation in our artificially designed world? The lucky ones will remember Matrix, the feminist design and architecture collective that was active during the 1980s and combined theory with practice through hands-on research in the field. They worked intensively with[in] communities via participatory methods, improved the built environment and women's engagement in the building

23

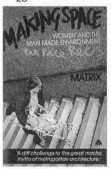

Matrix, *Making Space:
Women and the Man Made
Environment* (London:
Pluto Press, 1984).

24
There have been some
contemporary succes-
sors of *Matrix*, working
on a similar path and
methodology. FATALE,
Swedish-based feminist
research group on archi-
tecture and design (fatale-
architecture.blogspot.pt);
Women's Design Service
(www.wds.org.uk); and
taking place (takingplace.
org.uk) are not active anymore, while MUF, an art
and architecture collective
that implements feminism
subtly in public space (muf,
'An Invisible Privilege' in *Altering Practices: Feminist
Politics and Poetics of
Space*, ed. Doina Petrescu
[London and New York:
Routledge, 2007]); and
Barcelona-based Col-lectiu
Punt 6 (punt6.org) still
are. Each of these projects
made or still makes public
interventions through
participatory methods
and feminist agendas.

practices, and also provided technical support to communities. They also contextualized their practices and criticisms in written works, and in 1984, published a book entitled *Making Space: Women and the Man Made Environment.*[23] In this publication, through the theories of urban design, architecture and feminism, they elaborated on the systematic exclusion of women from public space and the dominance of male-oriented environments. Matrix was one of the vanguard groups that contributed to design theory and practice with a downright feminist discourse for the next generation of urban designers and architects.[24]

Then comes the gap. Although scholarly discussions and small-scale research projects in design schools continued and expanded into other new branches of design (e.g., Human-Computer Interaction [HCI], Science and Technology Studies (STS) and Game Design), the 1980s, 1990s and even the early 2000s have not witnessed many practice-based initiatives in this respect outside academia. Some remarkable examples are no older than a decade: Femme Den design lab, powered by Smart Design, based in the UK and US, has been active since 2006 and still develops design projects fulfilling the female users' needs. Opposing the commonplace products designed for women by the process of 'pinking and shrinking', they propound female-friendly products ranging from sports to housewares. Another three-year research project that finished in 2012, called 'Female Interaction', run by the Danish design company design-people, also focused on females as users of technology, and aimed to foster their interaction with innovative design artefacts such as smartphones, mobile apps and climate controllers. The Berlin-based Design Research Lab also ran several design research projects (including G-Gender Inspired Technology, Women's Phone and Gendered

Ece Canlı

Interfaces) for women as a neglected group, and by using participatory methods they designed apps and technologies fulfilling women's needs. In addition, the International Gender Design Network (IGDN) founded by Uta Brandes and Simone Douglas also supports events, knowledge exchange, and exploring practice and theory on the issues of gender and design.[25]

However, the 'gap' appears not only in the quantity of such projects but also in their contents. Although these groups have managed to challenge the subjugation of women in design and through designed things, their approach falls behind the contemporary discourse of gender. Since the 1980s, with third-wave feminism, along with sexuality studies, cultural theories, political philosophy and post-structural critiques, scholars have demonstrated how gender is only one thread of a greater 'matrix of domination'.[26] They claimed that hegemonic power and its oppression based on one's gender cannot be understood without understanding other identity constructions such as: sexuality, sexual orientation, race, ethnicity, class, religion, age, nationality, ability and so on, also known in the literature as intersectionality.[27] Meanwhile, queer theory, mainly evolved during the 1990s, not only debunked the stability of dichotomous gender and sex attributions (i.e. man/woman, female/male, feminine/masculine and hetero/homo), but embraced the plethora of non-conforming positions as places of the marginalized, disenfranchised, excluded, precarious and deviant bodies. Queer theory showed us that there are not just binary but miscellaneous genders and sexualities and that these identity categories are fluid as well. Last but not least, post-colonial-queer-feminist scholars more recently stressed that gender-based oppressions cannot be tackled as long as they are not seen as part of a colonial project strongly tied in with westernization,

25
www.femmeden.com; femaleinteraction.com/; genderdesign.org/; and www.design-research-lab.org, especially projects run by Sandra Buchmüller and Gesche Joost who have written extensively about the intersection of gender and design.

26
Patricia Hill Collins, *Black Feminist Thought: Knowledge, Consciousness, and the Politics of Empowerment* (New York: Routledge, 2000).

27
It emerged in the context of the black feminist movement and spread to many other disciplines. Coined by Kimberlé Crenshaw, 'Demarginalizing the Intersection of Race and Sex: A Black Feminist Critique of Antidiscrimination Doctrine, Feminist Theory and Antiracist Politics', *University of Chicago Legal Forum (PhilPapers)* 140 (1989), pp. 139–67.

modernism and capitalism—which are the 'fathers' of design. All in all, these critiques declare that without understanding the complexity of power structures, to counteract this status quo is no more impactful than sweeping the sands on the beach.

Looking at the contemporary feminist projects as mentioned above, a critical view shows that some elements are lacking, in terms of discourse around gender and feminist ideology. First and foremost, most of such works still deem 'woman' a monolithic category with a strong essentialism. Their concept of woman mostly equals to female, feminine, heterosexual, and, in some contexts, monogamous and mother; this eventually reproduces stereotypes about women, their 'taste', their technological abilities and their roles both in their public and domestic life. Moreover, the discourse of some of the projects is overtly based on companies' economic plans and therefore women remain, once again, potential consumers that would buy more gender-segregated products, but this time with 'feminist' concerns.[28] Meanwhile, a great percentage of the scholarly works and practices were or are based in the UK or the US, and few others in Western Europe. I am not favouring the 'feminism is the first world problem' aphorism here, nor do I underestimate their significant contributions to feminist struggle. I claim, however, that these projects run the risk of being ethnocentric, class-privileged and normative, since the targets, participants, doers and presenters of these projects are invariably white, hetero-cis-sexual,[29] [upper]middle-class, young and able-bodied. So, one may ask who is in the 'feminist-design' agenda and who is not, and according to what criteria? Is there a threshold for being unprivileged *enough*?

Besides, the scope of design is not limited to artefacts and their use, but belongs to a more complex sys-

28
For an analysis of some of the works from Femme Den and Female Interaction, see Ece Canlı, '[Non] Gendered Desires: Queer Possibilities in Design', *DESIGNA2014 Proceedings*, ed. Universidada da Beira Interior et al., p. 277–88 (Colvilhã: UBI, 2015), www.labcom-ifp.ubi. pt/ficheiros/201602151153-designa_2014_proceedings. pdf.

29
Cis or cisgender refers to people whose gender identity corresponds to their biological sex.

tem of manufacturing, dissemination and various forms of labour based on gender bias. Since the early 1980s, for instance, researchers have been revealing the exploitation of women working in Third World countries for multinational corporations. For the product, technology and fashion industries in particular, from Latin America to Asia, millions of young women, as the 'world's new industrial proletariat'[30] toil for inhuman working hours without insurance, safety, health considerations or sufficient wage. This multi-layered torment, which affects and is affected by gender, ethnicity, nationality, age and the like, is not only a socio-economic issue, but also of utmost interest to the design field. Therefore, the agenda of feminist-design urgently needs to be shifted from exclusive to expansive and subversive in ways that would challenge the existing *modus operandi* of design, its norms and misused privileges.

30
Barbara Ehrenreich and Annette Fuentes, 'Life on the Global Assembly Line', *Ms. Magazine* 9, no. 7 (January 1981), p. 52.

Need for a New Turn: Queer Agenda in Design

Now, I would like to take that good old question and re-modify it to 'Why have there been no queer-intersectional-decolonial-feminist design[ers]?', whereas mainstream culture, fashion , and areas such as visual and performing arts, literature, geography, and cultural studies have been already taken hold of a 'queer turn'. One of the possible answers would be the very status of design as a discipline that was born and spread from an already privileged position: Western, Euro-American-centric, white, male, heteronormative, prosperous, able, and the like. However, since this is also true of the fields mentioned above, other reasons may be the designers' over-concentration on object-oriented projects, the public image of these projects and of design itself, as well as their reluctance to move beyond the dichotomous gender discussion. As a result, they overlook the interconnectedness of all forms of identity-based oppressions and material power that overstep the limits of disciplinary interests. On the other hand, there have already been several research-led design works with an intriguing critical queer discourse on gender fluidity, non-binary sexual identity, and their possible reflections in designed materials. Some projects remain on the margins of art and design, but trying not to fall into the trap of the disciplinary divisions, I will stick to analysing the image, artefact and discourse production around gender, sexuality, identity, materiality, and visit some of them and their content.

Some of the best-known queer-feminist-oriented material works come from Zach Blas, creator of Queer Technologies, whose works humorously render the repressive implementation of technology, hegemonic surveillance and binary system of gender and sexuality dysfunctional. His works are significant not only contextually, but also in how he overturns the normative understanding of design that is functional, utilitarian, aesthetically charming and having use value. However, they do not serve as mere critical objects either, as in operating only as provocateurs, awareness-raisers or cultural mediators from the position of the bell jar; they actively confront the repressive technological regimes from within techno-material culture, in circulation. For instance, with the project ENgenderingGenderChangers,[31] he re-designed hardware connections in opposition to the existing binary connection system based on gender subordination and heterosexuality. Questioning the technology's strong association with gender and sexuality, he divulged the limits of interlockable female/male plugs and aimed to challenge users' perceptions on 'functionality, compatibility, and affordability' that sustain consumption and capitalist flow.[32] He proposed

31

Zach Blas, ENgendering Gender Changer, Queer Technologies, 2008.

32
users.design.ucla.edu/~z-blas/thesis_website/gender_changers/engendering_gender_changers.html.

Ece Canlı

WESTERNIZATION, MODERNISM, AND CAPITALISM

ARE THE 'FATHERS' OF THE DESIGN DESIGN THE DISCIPLINE

a wide range of gender adapters such as Male to Butch, Female to Power Bottom, Male to Femme, Male to Admin or Female to CEO to expand the complexity of IT solutions, beyond the sex bifurcation. Another work, Facial Weaponization Suite,[33] triggered by the worldwide social movements and protests that blasted in 2011, is an ongoing series of site-specific community workshops to disrupt racial recognition technologies. The work speaks out against governmental biometric standardizations that scan bodies and faces in airports, on borders or streets, yet put marginalized bodies at risk of being detected, caught, deported, fined or humiliated (e.g., immigrants, protesters, non-Caucasian faces, transgender people or people whose biological/certificated sex and facial gender presentation do not match). During the workshops, participants get their faces scanned and gather their different facial features into one single mask that is non-human, non-animal, distorted, and eventually uncatchable by biometric technologies. Alongside his other subversive works (transCoder, Gay Bombs), Blas interlaces intersectional queer theory, technology studies and practice not with a naive 'changing the world' platitude but for and through 'political desire, pedagogy, and collective experiences'.[34]

DE__SIGN, as another queer-driven practice-based research by Gabriel Ann Maher, holds design's media apparatuses such as magazines under the microscope. With that, Maher analyses critically how designed 'things' and the media that portray and disseminate them (i.e. magazines, websites, posters, video commercials) work hand in hand in repeating the cultural stereotypes and binary thinking about gender, sexuality, and thereby identity. By taking the Dutch design and architecture magazine *FRAME* as a case study, Maher analyses the representations of gendered and sexed

33

Zach Blas, Fag Face Mask, Facial Weaponization Suite, 2012.

34
www.vice.com/read/weaponizing-our-faces-an-interview-with-zach-blas-715, to be found at www.zachblas.info.

bodies in the magazine and reveals the problematic imagery and discourse embedded in various examples. Through visual deconstruction as a method—cutting out bodies from the pages and re-positioning them as montage—as well as by semantic analyses of the artefacts and their representations, DE__SIGN unfolds how the design practice is still conditioned and conditioning the dichotomous genders and sexualities, and cultural artefacts accordingly. Moreover, the project incorporates meticulous inspection of bodies of the colour and demonstrates the repetition of the colonial past to present that appears in stereotypical images of racial subordination and female sexuality. Finally, by problematizing the cultural codes of the body positions and their relation to gender and power dynamics, Maher focuses particularly on the sitting body. DE__SIGN: Act of Sitting, therefore, ensues as a material exploration and performance of some deconstructed postures and manifests the fluid ways of positioning the self.[35]

Another outstanding recent work was performed by the graphic designer, artist and queer-feminist activist Hélène Mourrier. She designed both the graphics and the content of the trans-formations booklets, *Ft** and *Mt**,[36] for and in collaboration with OUTrans, a non-profit feminist activist organization that supports transgender, FtM, MtF, as well as cisgendered individuals.[37] Being strongly involved with trans-feminist activism and well-informed with the surgical and scientific terms; Mourrier designed the catalogues that illustrate gender reassignment processes for transgender people as still one of the most marginalized, isolated, and disenfranchised group in society. Merging the medical lexicon with her own political queer discourse, anatomic shapes with her own graphic aesthetics, she provided a piece of work reflecting a hybrid corpus, a 'knowledge in resistance'.[38] In her detailed illustrations

35
Gabriel Ann Maher, 'De__Sign: Revealing the Condition of the Mediated Body', in *The Virtuous Circle: Design Culture and Experimentation: Proceedings of the Cumulus Conference, June 3–7, Milan*, ed. Luisa Collina, Laura Galluzzo and Anna Meroni, pp. 1051–65 (Milan: Unitec, 2015). For the *DE__SIGN-Act of Sitting*, see vimeo.com/109313338.

36
outrans.org/docs/FT_.pdf and outrans.org/docs/MT_.pdf.

37
FtM refers to 'Female to Male', while MtF 'Male to Female' gender reassignment, mostly through surgical processes. In Mourrier's work, *Ft** and *Mt** signify 'Fe/male to Something', not taking gender codes for granted and already de-stabilizing them.

38
Tiphaine Kazi-Tani. 'Queer Graphics. The Critical Work of Hélène Mourrier' *ENVELOPE* *2015: Designing Critical Messages, Plymouth, United Kingdom* (Plymouth: Plymouth University, 2015), p. 2, halshs.archives-ouvertes.fr/halshs-01120242/document.

Ece Canlı

of body parts involved in the transition process, she uses quadratic and geometric shapes and smooth pastel colours in contrast with overtly depictive, realistic and exhibitory medical imagery. Also, her use of flesh-like warm pink puts the erotic and sexual aspects in question, as an implicit reminder that trans bodies are also for sex and love. Eluding the mere representation of a highly delicate matter, Mourrier's work introduces design's political dimension with(in) queer discourse, as well as its practical implementation specifically for the outcasts and bodies on the fringes.

As to the subject of graphic design, gender segregation, sexuality and designed environments, today many people are aware of public toilets, not only with regard to their spatial divisions but also their pictogrammic references. Compared to other material artefacts, signage systems and spaces, bathrooms have been extensively and frequently discussed by queer theoreticians, activists, scholars and practitioners. However, every day people are subjected to verbal or physical violence for 'misusing' public bathrooms as a result of their non-conforming gender presentations and sexual orientations. Genderpoo[39] is a queer-graphic work about bathroom signs being carried out by Coco Guzman—a.k.a. Coco Riot—since 2008, as a manifestation against normalcy of bodies. Based on simple but sophisticated vector-based drawings, the work grows through participants in workshops as an assemblage of miscellaneous deviant, mutant and monster-like bodies that confront the ideal form of anatomy and identity presentation. A mermaid with breasts and moustache,[40] two skirted-figures in sixty-nine position, a nun peeing standing up, a hairy protestor with Molotov cocktail and veil, or a brunette amputee dissident not only depict myriad forms of gender and sexuality, but also put other biased and

39
www.cocoriot.com/gender-poo/, www.youtube.com/watch?v=ViZvtA0j4K0.

40

Coco Riot (Coco Guzman), Sirena, Genderpoo, 2008.

marginalized identity categories in question. Moreover, the project was not limited to pictorial experimentations, but also spread to other material forms such as garments, publications and the physical façades of bathrooms, as other examples for multiple material modifications.

Last but not least, design researcher Luiza Prado de O. Martins takes a closer look at the politics of contraceptive pills and their historicity from an intersectional and decolonial point of view. Considering pills as designed artefacts, she examines not only their role in controlling bodies' gender (presentation) and reproductive functions through hormonal manipulations, but also their partaking in taming and restraining raced and classed sexuality. Her theoretically rich work blooms with the new methodologies and participatory workshops where she scrutinizes the direct effects of material artefacts on our material bodies through anachronistic processes of history-re-making.[41]

As can be seen from the examples, a queer turn in design does not mean 'design for queer people' as a new marketplace for production or to make an inventory of 'queer designers'.[42] Nor does it regard queerness in design as a stylistic umbrella for all marginalized identities or merely being genderless or 'unisex'. A queer turn, however, is first to acknowledge design's direct and ruthless impacts on people based on artefactual, spatial, sartorial or digital segregations; and, in turn, how bodies reiterate and reactivate the meanings embedded in these materials by performing, embodying or inhabiting them every day. Therefore, new generation queer-feminist protagonists of design will undertake several challenging tasks: bearing in mind that design is a material form of dominant power, they must constantly call design's intentions and outcomes into question, deconstruct its exclusionary and oppressive modes and unceasingly re-politicize it.

41
Luiza Prado de O. Martins, 'Pills, genders and design: Speculations on Queer Materialities' (2015), www. academia.edu/24586798/ Pills_genders_and_design_ Speculations_on_Queer_ Materialities.

42
As it started in architecture since the 1990s, as the project of bringing architects' sexualities into sight, mostly explicitly closeted ones, such as furniture designer and architect Eileen Gray.

Ece Canlı

An urge for a queer turn is not to call for a new trend or a movement in design for the sake of design. Nor is it a linear progression from feminism. It is a project of excavating, unfolding and unravelling the hegemonies of a material practice deeply entrenched in our cultural, social, and daily contexts. Some design projects speculate about possible dystopias and use designed artefacts to raise awareness about what may happen in the future. However, as many design scholars already pointed out, this dystopia happens right now, in many places to many people, in real life.[43] So, a queer turn is also a project of turning this dystopia into utopian imaginations instead of bogging down in an inert cynicism, and using design to counteract itself.

To observe the proliferation of today's designed artefacts that target gender and sexuality–such as the ones listed in the beginning of this essay–is certainly thought-provoking. However, it is important to keep a wary eye on the inclusive guise of profit-oriented productions and to remember that every inclusion means someone else's exclusion, if not persecution. A genuine queer-feminist agenda is to construe the historical, political and material aspects of sex, gender, and other identity discrimination and contextualize them carefully within larger power structures.

History is already being written; it is not an irreversible past, but an extricable today. Thus, instead of waiting for reclaiming or re-writing another history in the future, the queer-feminist-design agenda should interrupt the ongoing history here and now, load it with anti-hegemonic, intersectional, and decolonial discourses and criticisms, make it even 'messier'. I believe that it might be one of the ways to resist oppressive, discriminatory and 'neat' material power, and to turn design and its history from a patchwork to a queer amalgam.

43
Scholars such as Cameron Tonkinwise, Ahmed Ansari, Luiza Prado de O. Martins, Pedro J. S. Vieira de Oliveira and Matt Kiem have written critically about this issue.

The Digital Age Reaches the Fringes
A Public Fab Lab in Brazil and Its (Possible) Implications for Design

Andrea Bandoni

Digital fabrication is blooming in Brazil through massive media diffusion, government support and a growing number of Fab Labs (Fabrication Laboratories)—these being a network of laboratories with high tech machines, such as 3D printers and laser cutters, present all over the world. At a time when mass production is being challenged by the possibility of personal fabrication adjusted to local conditions, a lot of expectations about the future are raised by a new Fab Lab in the periphery of São Paulo, since this area has a lot of needs and Fab Lab ideals are highly democratic. Facing issues such as technology advancements, authorship in the digital age, new environments and ways of working, designers are given the chance to be the protagonists of a possible social and cultural change, as long as they understand and assume their role and responsibilities in finding coherent ways of developing the specific contexts within which they act.

March 2016 – A great month for digital fabrication in São Paulo. Eight new free access Fab Labs opened across the city, almost all of them in peripheral neighbourhoods. In addition, the major public access TV channel in Brazil started broadcasting a special series in its Sunday night programming called *Fab Lab: Do it Yourself*, showing the ideals of this movement and concentrating on the solutions dedicated especially to the poor, such as a low-cost hand prosthesis for a child, scientific lab tools for a public school, and an electrical bike to be used on the favela's slopes. But it was not always like that.

This story starts somewhere in 2011, when a small group of design and architecture researchers who were interested in digital fabrication started meeting at the Faculty of Architecture at the University of São Paulo, Brazil. Although they were aware of the advancements

Andrea Bandoni

in technology and contemporary design, by that time few of the participants of that selected group had had the chance to work with or even see most of the innovative tools being researched, such as 3D printers.

This group wanted to gain a better understanding of the potential of digital fabrication and to connect with other existing Labs, especially in Latin America. Therefore it was necessary to first have a Lab in order to experiment with the new machines and techniques and to make it available to a broader audience. The best example at that point was the Fab Lab Uni, which had just opened in Lima, Peru, and made it seem possible to have such a Lab in Brazil as well.

It is not difficult to understand why Fab Labs held such an appeal to this Brazilian group and why this model was adopted with such confidence. A Fab Lab is a platform for rapid prototyping of physical objects, embedded in a global network that is constantly growing (now approaching 650 labs[1]). Moreover, the fact that this idea was born in the Massachusetts Institute of Technology (MIT), USA, made the initiative seem very reliable.

1
According to www.fablabs.io/labs (accessed 26 April 2016).

Fab Lab Ideals and Context

Neil Gershenfeld is a physicist and Director of the MIT's Center for Bits and Atoms (CBA), where the boundary between computer science and physical science is studied. In 1998, he offered a university course with the title 'How to Make Almost Anything' that fostered the use of digital fabrication machines:

> We designed the class to teach a small group of research students how to use CBA's tools but were overwhelmed by the demand from students who just wanted to make things.[2]

2
Neil Gershenfeld, 'How to Make Almost Anything: The Digital Fabrication Revolution', *Foreign Affairs* 91, no. 6 (November-December 2012), p. 46.

Because of its success, after a few years this project was developed into the idea of maintaining a continuous Lab for 'making things' outside MIT; this is how the first Fab Lab was born, in 2003. It made publicly available a space with a set of equipment with minimum cost but still beyond what individuals could afford, including a computer-controlled laser cutter, a 3D printer, and large and small computer-controlled milling machines.

This permanent Lab with high-end technologies for local and individual production, where new things and even new machines could be developed, was based on an idealistic democratization of the latest means of production, as science and technology researchers Julia Walter-Herrmann and Corinne Büching write:

> From the outset, Gershenfeld's fundamental idea was not only *to make almost anything* but to make fabrication technologies accessible for *almost anybody* and hence empower people to start their own technological futures.[3]

3
Julia Walter-Herrmann, and Corinne Büching, 'Notes on Fab Labs', in *Fab Lab: Of Machines, Makers and Inventors*, ed. Julia Walter-Herrmann and Corinne Büching (Wetzlar: Transcript, 2013), p. 13.

Social empowerment certainly happens in Fab Labs, possibly thanks to the values embedded in the network. These values are protected by a document named Fab Charter and by the Fab Foundation, an organization that supports the growth of the international Fab Lab network. The principles laid down in the Fab Charter clearly focus on the 'sharing' aspect of the labs and on benefiting communities rather than companies. For example, it states that one of the responsibilities of the users is to document and provide instructions about their work, and also that commercial activities can take place within the lab but must never conflict with other uses and should benefit the ones who contribute to these activities. For the Fab Foundation, one criterion to

Andrea Bandoni

qualify as a Fab Lab is 'first and foremost, public access to the Fab Lab .... A Fab Lab is about democratizing access to the tools for personal expression and invention'.[4]

A simple and easy to understand Lab model—which provides access to technology combined with a multidisciplinary network, that is encouraged to stay connected, document, share and learn from past projects – is part of the reason why Fab Labs started spreading around the world over the past thirteen years and why they could so readily adapt to so many different cultures, including that of Brazil. Another reason for Fab Lab's success is a broader change that global society is undergoing. Researcher Peter Troxler, who has published extensively on open source technology, argues that

> Undoubtedly, developments in manufacturing technology will play an important role in the next industrial revolution. Yet the main disruption that the next industrial revolution will bring is the disruption of hierarchical systems and the emergence of systems of lateral power.[5]

In *Making the Third Industrial Revolution* Troxler mentions three authors that invoked this new revolution: Gershenfeld, who focuses on the diffusion of new means for production, journalist Chris Anderson, who sees this new revolution as the combination of digital and personal manufacturing, and economist and writer Jeremy Rifkin, who points out that the internet, renewable energy, and distributed manufacturing may shift the way society is structured: from hierarchical power towards lateral power. According to them, the extraordinary democratization of information which the Internet has enabled is about to be mirrored by

4
Fab Foundation, 'The Fab Charter', 2015, www.fabfoundation.org/fab-labs/the-fab-charter (accessed 26 April 2016).

5
Peter Troxler, 'Making the Third Industrial Revolution', in *Fab Lab: of Machines, Makers and Inventors*, ed. Julia Walter-Herrmann and Corinne Büching (Wetzlar: Transcript, 2013), p. 181.

the democratization of physical creation. As manufacturing goes digital and production processes become easier to access, the era of mass production is put into question. Customization and smaller scales can now become the norm, changing the world of creation, production and distribution but also that of consumption and waste.

Fab Labs and Design: Ethics, Aesthetics, Authorship

Design critic Alice Rawsthorn observes that 'having enjoyed the benefits of standardization for so long, we take them for granted, and yearn for idiosyncrasy' and adds 'we are increasingly eager to take the design decisions ourselves, rather than delegating them to designers'.[6] Maybe this explains the reason behind the success of Neil Gershenfeld's seminal class 'How to Make Almost Anything', when his students started to explore the digital techniques. Gershenfeld mentions that he was surprised by the fact that the students were answering a question that he had not asked: 'What is digital fabrication good for? As it turns out, the "killer app" in digital fabrication, as in computing, is personalization, producing products for a market of one person'.[7]

Of course personalization is not new: it was the norm before the industrial era and it is still the way things are being produced in many parts of the planet where industry did not completely replace craft manufacture, including several locations in Brazil. The difference is that the access to new technologies can now make mass customization possible, which means that many more people will have the chance to make and to have their own unique products, wherever they are. These new disrupting technologies inspire a belief that

6
Alice Rawsthorn, *Hello World: Where Design Meets Life* (London: Penguin Books, 2013), pp. 193–95.

7
Gershenfeld, 'How to Make Almost Anything', pp. 46–47.

Andrea Bandoni

DYSTOPIA HAPPENS RIGHT NOW, IN MANY

if their implementation is well managed, then people's needs can be fulfilled locally in a much less harmful way than before with mass-consumerism industries, which led to massive destruction of nature, pollution and waste. Although this is not yet proven by Fab Labs, there are a few projects experimenting in that direction, such as The Amazon Floating Fab Lab, an ongoing project that aims to

> provide local communities with access to technological tools that allow them to cope with their daily challenges with water, energy, health, food, education while at the same time, serve as a place for research and development to better understand the Amazon[8]

Surely, these technologies open up doors for more research since the costs of testing new products are much lower than in standardized factories, and this alone can have a significant impact on the design world, both aesthetically and ethically.

Besides a new language that originated in digital modelling techniques and is being explored in contemporary objects mostly by designers,[9] we now have production of objects on a massive scale in the maker spaces. Corinne Büching analysed the objects produced in workshops conducted at Fab Lab St. Pauli in Hamburg, Germany, in terms of two categories: *objects to download* (from open source archives available through websites such as Thingiverse) and *home-made objects* (constructed digitally by the maker or user themselves). According to Büching,

> the fascination we have with the things that are created in Fab Labs can be traced back to their being self-made, new and having a personal

8
Amazon Floating Fab Lab, 2014, amazon.fablat.org/en/fab-flotante-amazonas (accessed 26 April 2016).

9
'The work of OpenStructures, Unfold and other design groups committed to developing new ways of working with new production technologies suggests that the surreal aesthetic of 3D printing will also be adept at reflecting the cultural shift away from the twentieth-century illusion of clarity and uniformity by expressing the contradictions and inconsistencies of human nature (...)' Rawsthorn, *Hello World*, pp. 200–1.

meaning. They express individuality and creativity and encourage the users to continue crafting.[10]

However, if, on the one hand, personalization brings attachment to objects, on the other hand, a visit to a Fab Lab can show that many of the things that are digitally constructed and built in these places today are useless artefacts that are sometimes also distributed through the internet. Creation and materialization are definitely important aspects of the maker culture, but they are not always made with much awareness. Not everyone is conscious of what it takes to introduce new things into this world: the cycle of the materials, the costs of the processes, the life span of the objects, and so on. Perhaps the emotional ties brought by customization, local production, and digital machines with low energy costs may balance the impact of barely designed pieces built with non-sustainable materials. However, even if digital fabrication is something new, meaningful and valuable today, what guarantees do we have that in a few years these objects will still have their 'aura' in order to be adored and kept? And what implications does this have for the future? Maybe this signals one of the responsibilities of designers in these new maker environments: to show alternatives and design strategies that can help in minimizing harm.

Even though designers can be valuable to environments of makers, paradoxically, not all of them may be flexible enough to adapt to the DIY and maker worlds. In terms of authorship, the mindset in the universe of Fab Labs is based on the collaboration of multidisciplinary teams (co-creation) and in 'openness' for exchanging information.[11] 'Open design' is a term commonly described as the development of physical products through the use of publicly shared information[12] and

10
Corinne Büching, 'A Universe of Objects', in *Fab Lab: of Machines, Makers and Inventors*, ed. Julia Walter-Herrmann and Corinne Büching (Wetzlar: Transcript, 2013), p. 116.

11
Designer Heloisa Neves, a core supporter of the development of the Fab Lab movement in Brazil, in the conclusion of her PhD thesis *Maker Innovation* mentions that 'collaboration' and 'openness' are the two most powerful concepts that arise from her analysis of strategies used by the maker movement.

12
This definition comes from Wikipedia defined by design researchers Meroz and Griffin 'arguably an authoritative reference in this context'. Joana Ozorio de Almeida Meroz and Rachel Griffin, 'Open Design: A History of the Construction of a Dutch Idea', in *Pruys Bekaert 2014*, ed. Archined and Designplatform Rotterdam, 2014, p. 28, www.ontwerpschrijfkunst.org/wp/wp-content/uploads/2013/09/OSK-web-pub-secure.pdf (accessed on 26 April 2016).

Andrea Bandoni

this concept is implicit in the Fab Foundation's website:

> Who owns fab lab inventions? Designs and processes developed in fab labs can be protected and sold however an inventor chooses, but should remain available for individuals to use and learn from.[13]

13
Fab Foundation. 'The Fab Charter'.

Although it may not seem to be a problem at first, this distinct way of working puts into question design's conventional way of generating income, either through royalties or by producing exclusive products for companies/clients in closed contracts. Will designers be able to reinvent their profession? Are they really willing to be part of an environment where the system has a non-traditional configuration? What are the designer's goals and interests in these places? These questions have to be addressed in order to understand design's potential in an emerging scene across the world.

A Fab Lab in the Periphery: Success or Failure?

One of the primary goals in implementing Fab Labs in Brazil was to have digital tools and spaces for experimentation. That would be the basics to start with, yet, since there are so many urgent agendas in Brazil, it took the initial group a while to figure out that this project had to become part of these 'Brazilian urgent agendas' in order to exist. 'Design' in itself would not be enough of an argument, but innovation, digital manufacturing, democratization of technologies, and creative industry development along with other possibilities inherent to Fab Labs, could help the project catch on—as ultimately happened.

Although Fab Labs took a while to arrive in Brazil

14
According to
www.fablabs.io/labs
(accessed 26 April 2016)
there are 17 Fab Labs in
Brazil. Adding the 12 new
São Paulo's Free Access
Fab Labs there are 29 in
total.

15
More information can be
found on documents of
the call for this 2015 contest, in which the winner
was a company named
'Its Brasil': e-negociosci-
dadesp.prefeitura.sp.gov.
br/DetalheLicitacao.aspx-
?l=RXgb05efqrl%3d.

16
This visit was on March
2016.

3D printer at Fab Lab
Tiradentes, photo by
Andrea Bandoni, 2016.

Laser cutter at Fab Lab
Tiradentes, photo by
Andrea Bandoni, 2016.

(the first Brazilian Fab Lab opened in 2011, years after India and many African countries), they found fertile ground here.[14] In 2012, a new mayor was elected in São Paulo who promised drastic changes, and one of the items in his agenda was that of digital inclusion. In 2014, his team came across the Fab Lab model and ideals, and understood the impact it could have on society— and on his government. São Paulo's free access digital fabrication program, Fab Lab Livre SP, was then conceived, and it started with a public contest in which the winning company would take responsibility for the machines, staff and programme implementation. The new Labs were to be established inside the existing municipal cultural centre buildings located all over the city, including those in peripheral neighbourhoods.[15]

This is how Fab Lab Tiradentes, the first of such Labs, was established by the end of 2015. It takes around two hours by public transport to get from the centre of São Paulo to the community of Cidade Tiradentes where it is located. During this trip, the scenery changes abruptly from high-rise buildings to repetitive blocks of social housing and favelas. The shift is not only visual, of course, but also economic, educational, and cultural.

Since Fab Lab Tiradentes is the pioneer and sits in such a remote part of the city, it creates a lot of expectations. However, once you arrive there,[16] it becomes clear that it will take a while before local people will make this idealistic project their own. The Lab is a beautiful space inside a not-so-new cultural centre that offers various activities but is often not very busy. And since the Fab Lab was not requested by the people themselves, it still has to prove its worth: even with all the good intentions of São Paulo's municipality, locals do not seem to need the Lab so far. There are few activities being proposed in this Fab Lab and most of

Andrea Bandoni

them take place in the afternoon, which is not the best time for people from Cidade Tiradentes since many work in São Paulo's centre. To reach a larger audience, this Fab Lab will have to reschedule their activities to the evening hours and weekends. The place is run by monitors who have to implement classes and ateliers defined by the company that runs all of the Fab Lab Livre's network. As some of these monitors are still in training, certain machines are currently not in use. At the moment, potential Fab Lab users are mostly curious children, a few of whom are already developing their own objects, such as 3D printed ear stretchers for their own use.

At this point, there is a feeling that Fab Labs like Tiradentes can be a failure if their 'social animators' are not trained well enough and just keep on replicating already existing objects instead of realizing the project's full potential. On the other hand, these Fab Labs can become a huge success when embedded in their context and people spontaneously participate and propose activities. As Fab Labs provide new means for local self-expression, the hope is that they will help in solving local issues and revealing local culture, thereby treating the periphery as a centre in its own right. They can provide the opportunity for many more people to discover themselves as makers, bio hackers, designers, engineers, and artists. Then Fab Lab Tiradentes could become a window of opportunities, a symbol of change. Yet, how to catalyse this identity and make things happen within a strong, pre-defined context?

Possible Happy Endings for Digital Fabrication in Brazil

Taking Brazil in its totality, the first thing about identity

A project that goes in that direction was 'Objects of the Forest', 2012 by Andrea Bandoni. It consisted in a design expedition in the Amazon region to find sustainable materials and solutions still existing there. Its findings are shared in a blog and e-book: objetosdafloresta. com/download.

18
Karin Zindel, 'Field Trip to Brazil: Design Lab Brazil: Learning from the Informal', 2015. master.design. zhdk.ch/news/design-lab-brazil-learning-from-the-informal (accessed 26 April 2016).

19

Gambiarra: barbecue skewer on a wheelbarrow and chair, photo by Cao Guimarães, 2000–2014.

Gambiarra: mudguard made from a plastic bottle.

that comes to mind is its immense cultural and material diversity, which is often excluded from design or any other practices. Especially when we think about materials and nature, there are so many underexplored or even unknown things here that it will take ages of dedicated work to figure them out. In the digital age, researching and exploring these natural materials, their traditional uses and techniques is not only a way to establish local connections but also a path to new possibilities in design.[17] The combination of biomaterials, digital fabrication, and maker strategies could definitely generate consistent and responsible proposals for the future.

When the context is the periphery of São Paulo, the focus changes from nature to urban adaptation. Design Researcher Karin Zindel, from the Zürcher Hochschule der Künste in Zurich, in a call for participation in her 2015 expedition 'Design Lab Brazil: Learning from the Informal' that aimed to explore the man-made environment through urban walks writes:

> For more than decades, a hardly noticed, but particular design form originating from existential needs, limited economic resources, as well as from the local and cultural context of individuals living in precarious conditions in urban centres, has been an integral part of developing or industrially less developed countries. This kind of design has, at the same time, been the result of an individual survival strategy and the expression of a collective improvisational spirit, and has by these means filled a niche in the local non-official economic system.[18]

The identities of these less developed localities are definitely affected by adaptive strategies, and in Brazil the best-known of them is a practice that has similarities to *bricolage* and to *hacking*: the *gambiarra*,[19] a spontaneous method of repairing and creating things. Brazilian curator and researcher Gabriel Menotti mentions that

> *Gambiarra* is an improvised amendment to a dysfunctional artefact, normally by the means of its combination with another object. One of the most exemplary gambiarras is the use of wire wool in TV antennas to compensate deficient signal reception. ... To recover function, the superficial individuality of the artefact must be sacrificed. Simultaneously, another object reveals potentials that were not expected.[20]

Typically regarded by everyone in Brazil with a negative bias because it is born from the failure of an artefact, *gambiarra* nevertheless has interesting parallels with the maker world. The improvement of objects brings it closer to open design practices, in which the *development* of the original object is not only accepted,[21] but sometimes is even a sign of success because it shows someone can solve a problem with whatever is around at the moment. A next step would be to publicly share *gambiarras* on the internet and preferably for free, something that is already informally being done on several Brazilian websites and social networks.[22]

Improvisation and necessity present in this kind of simple solutions seem to be a powerful match to Fab Lab ideals, and could introduce better use of the means that exist in these places, as Brazilian cultural entrepreneur Felipe Fonseca writes:

> In the context of a contemporary society struggling for sustainability, meaning, creativity and

20
Gabriel Menotti, 'Gambiarra: the prototyping perspective': Paper presented at the Interactivos?'10: Neighborhood Science workshop, Media Lab Prado – Madrid, June 7–23, 2010, medialab-prado.es/article/gambiarra.

21
As design researchers Joana Meroz and Rachel Griffin mention: 'As in the free and open source software movements before it, the internet facilitates the sharing of data, allowing other individuals to copy or evolve the original object. ... This pool of shared data forms the commons, a body of information freely available for public use. Thus, where once methods of production were highly centralized in large, hierarchical corporations, this data-sharing coupled with new technologies proposes a new decentralized, grassroots, bottom-up production model.' Meroz and Griffin, 'Open Design', p. 28.

22
Some websites: somentecoisaslegais.com.br/curiosidades/7-gambiarras-mais-comuns-da-familia-brasileira and www.buzzfeed.com/manuelabarem/gambiarras-que-falam-mais-sobre-a-alma-do-brasileiro-do-q?utm_term=.dr8DYPQOX#.lt09Gxvem. For more details check Rodrigo Boufleur, 'A Questão da Gambiarra: Formas alternativas de desenvolver artefatos e suas relações com o design de produtos', master's diss.

22 (cont.)
University of São Paulo, 2006, www.teses.usp.br/teses/disponiveis/16/ 16134/tde-24042007-150223/pt-br.php, and gambiarra images by photographer Cao Guimarães, www.caoguimaraes.com/foto/gambiarras.

23
Felipe Fonseca, *Repair Culture*, 2015, efeefe.no-ip.org/livro/re-pair-culture/ (accessed 26 April 2016).

value, *gambiarra* seems to have more to offer than the weak existence of layers and layers of plastic-made prototypes.[23]

A culture of reusing, hacking, repairing, and re-purposing objects appears to be more in line with the local possibilities and habits of São Paulo's periphery than producing brand new things with an imported aesthetics. The mix between *gambiarra* and digital devices in the post-industrial era may have surprising results that the design world could learn from and blend with. It is essential, then, that those more traditional practices become valued, and that they resist the pressure of mass markets that nowadays tend to quash them. In order to bring to life all the changes and revolutions that are expected, it seems crucial that the latest digital means of production adopt significant local features, so that they can be more than a trend and become part of the culture and an inherent motor of a new age.

Andrea Bandoni

If Not Tomorrow, Then Today
Paradigms of Latin American Design

Luiza Prado de O. Martins &
Pedro J. S. Vieira de Oliveira

Adding to the renewed wave of interest in social innovation design in Latin America from the early to mid-
twenty-first century, the exhibition '¡Hubla! Ayer y Hoy:
Los Paradigmas del Diseño Social Latinoamericano'
focuses on the activities of the Latin American Hub for
Innovation in Social Design.[1] Established as a multinational public-private partnership, the Hub had branches
in two large cities in the Southern Cone—Valparaíso
(Chile) and Buenos Aires (Argentina), plus another
one in Brasília (Brazil). Yet, during its twenty-plus-year
long existence, ¡Hubla! actively worked with projects,
services, and workshops all around Latin America.
This particular exhibition, curated by design historians
Marta Rodríguez-Guayra and Sebastian Brengartner,
which was held in the Main Exhibition Hall of the Pan-
american Council for Social Design in New York City,
was the first one to showcase a comprehensive collection of the Hub's work, and hence provided a much
needed glimpse into a complex web of power, politics,
and technology in the continent—albeit, at times,
unintentionally.

In order to understand the projects developed by
the Hub during this period, one must first understand
the context within which they were conceived; sadly,
the exhibition does a poor job contextualizing the
historical, social, cultural, political, and economic environment that shaped these artefacts. There is little
or no mention of any implications and consequences
of these projects other than those that fit the success
narrative of the Hub. Consequently, the shifting political
scenarios faced by the continent during the time that
¡Hubla! was at its creative peak are often flattened out
to storytelling that relies too much on techno-solution-
ism, and praise for the wonders of technological development in times of political conservatism. Considering
that the curatorial statement suggested, in so many

1

The exhibition's name in
English: '¡Hubla! Yesterday
and Today: The Paradigms
of Latin American Social
Design', February 17–July
27. In Spanish the Hub is
called 'Hub Latinoamer-
icano de Innovación en
Diseño Social', also informally known as '¡Hubla!'.

Luiza Prado de O. Martins & Pedro J. S. Vieira de Oliveira

words, an intent to dissect the social implications of the Hub's activities during the years of political turmoil preceding and following its foundation, such an uncritical celebration seems a glaring omission.

In the following pages we aim to provide a critical review of the exhibition, addressing these shortcomings by looking at projects that we feel are able to illustrate the numerous aspects of social innovation design and its relationship to Latin American politics. Rather than provide an overview of the many projects and prototypes available in the exhibition, our analysis and contextualization will instead go deeper into two specific instances: 'Ruídografías'—a week-long workshop carried out simultaneously in five large cities in three different countries—and Oníria, a fertility-tracking product developed as the result of a collaboration between ¡Hubla! and pharmaceutical conglomerate TZPharma.

Design and the Politics of Fertility: The Case of Oníria

At the time of ¡Hubla!'s establishment, contraception and reproductive health had been, for decades, an extremely lucrative market in Latin America. Regulatory systems for contraceptives were, however, changing; abortion had long been a contentious issue in the continent, with most countries (Uruguay being a notable exception) defining it as a crime in their constitution or criminal code. Most countries tolerated only very few cases in which an abortion would be permitted—such as immediate risk to the woman's life, or rape. Granted, even in these cases it was a rare occurrence for an abortion to be actually performed: the bureaucratic process for securing this right was long and gatekeepers (e.g., police officers or hospital staff) were frequently uncooperative.

Blurring the boundaries between contraception and abortion, a number of increasingly strict reproductive health policies were adopted by many Latin American countries (most notably Brazil, Colombia, and Chile) in the early 2000s. Life, lawmakers concluded, began at conception; as such, it followed that abortion was a crime against life. Brazil's 'Estatuto do Nascituro' (Statute of the Unborn) and Chile's 'Derecho de Nacimiento' (Right to be Born) bills went a step further, however: both framed medications such as the morning-after pill or birth control pills, as well as medical devices such as IUDs, as abortive methods. Use of these contraceptives was, from then on, banned; as a consequence, alternative methods—especially those based on fertility awareness—started gaining traction, marketed as natural and healthy family planning strategies.

In order to adapt to these new policies and maintain profit margins, pharmaceutical companies had no choice but to invest heavily in the research and development of new products. It is within this context that ¡Hubla! partnered with TZPharma to provide the assistance and expertise in the design of a product adapted to these new realities; thus Oníria, a wearable fertility-tracking device, was born. The product's function was not entirely new: other fertility-tracking products had already been available in the market for some years. However, this project represented an important milestone for !Hubla! due to its significant size and broad scope. TZPharma is a pharmaceutical conglomerate whose subsidiaries had, in previous years, struck public-private partnership deals with the governments of Brazil, Colombia, and Chile. With new contraception laws being passed in all three countries, the parent

Luiza Prado de O. Martins & Pedro J. S. Vieira de Oliveira

THE NEXT INDUSTRIAL REVOLUTION WILL BRING THE DISRUPTION OF

HIERARCHICAL SYSTEMS AND THE EMERGENCE OF LATERAL POWER

company turned to the Hub for the necessary (i.e. designerly) expertise in developing a solution to maintain a firm hold on the contraceptives market.

Oníria is a cheap, viable solution for fertility management, meant to be distributed by the public health systems of all three countries. Unlike other fertility-tracking devices (which tended to resemble discrete band-aids fitted with sensors), Oníria is designed to resemble a small piece of jewellery to be worn in the mouth at night, in order to track basal body temperature (BBT).[2] Its shape is faintly reminiscent of some sort of U-shaped clip meant to be worn between the internal and external parts of the mouth, straddling the labial commissure. The object's inner tip sits on the inner cheek and is fitted with a highly sensitive thermometer, used for measuring not only basal body temperature but also a significant number of other data, from hormonal levels to immunologic health. The sensor is encased in a soft, thin, rubbery shell, designed to be as unobtrusive as possible inside the mouth. The data collected by this sensor is then automatically sent to the woman's health care provider, allegedly as a strategy to prevent patients from self-medicating. Effectively, it is a design that places control over one's reproductive cycle in the hands of gatekeepers—be it private health care providers, or the public health system—instead of in the hands of the 'patient' herself.

Oníria's external tip would sit in near the cheekbone and was, in its first prototypes, rather bare in terms of embellishments and design features.[3] Throughout the development and user-testing of the product, designers at ¡Hubla! noticed that forgetfulness was an issue, as BBT tracking needs to be done with regularity; furthermore, several users had complained about the visible marks left on their cheeks by sleeping with the contraption. The solution for these problems was as

2
Basal body temperature is the lowest temperature attained during the sleep cycle; during ovulation, body temperature shows a small, but sharp increase and thus its tracking can be used to determine fertility.

3

First commercial model for Oníria.

unorthodox as it was successful: instead of creating a more comfortable product, Oníria's outer tip was entirely redesigned, so that the marks it left on the face would be more enticing.

To ensure effectiveness, an aggressive marketing campaign followed, promoting the marks left by Oníria on one's cheeks as a coveted status symbol, a marker of moral values—femininity, chastity, and heterosexuality—and, abstinence having become the accepted norm, social and marital status. The product was prominently placed in telenovelas and worn by characters with whom women identified more strongly; it was also sent out to influential internet personalities for review and publicity, and largely discussed (and praised) on morning TV shows. Oníria was ¡Hubla!'s first and perhaps biggest success: trendsetters began using makeup in order to mimic or highlight the effect of these marks on the cheek; countless video tutorials[4] describing how to emulate these marks can still be found online. The product effectively shifted how fertility awareness products were designed and marketed; other manufacturers soon followed suit with more elaborate designs, capable of imprinting intricate patterns on the wearer's cheek, or expensive, custom-made versions made out of high-end materials and inlaid with small gems.

The exhibition unfortunately fails to provide this kind of context for the development of Oníria; as a consequence, important discussions on the object's social, political, and cultural impact are either glossed over, or downright silenced. Unquestionably, Oníria and the products developed after it played a pivotal role in shaping Latin America's approach to reproductive health. Yet, throughout the exhibition there is no mention of the flawed tracking system in first generation products, identified after a data leak in a hospital in

4

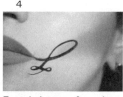

Found picture of a make-up tutorial by once-famous beauty blogger Fabíola Tedeschi. In this tutorial she teaches how to highlight the marks left by 'Love' , a special edition of the original Oníria sent by the Hub exclusively to digital influencers like her, for review and advertisement purposes. The size of the swirls is a strong character of this edition, and symbolizes a woman's fidelity to her husband.

Luiza Prado de O. Martins & Pedro J. S. Vieira de Oliveira

Medellín, Colombia, which led to a series of problems for patients. There is no discussion on how these devices played a central role in campaigns aiming to limit the reproductive rights of recipients of social benefits in Brazil, or how lower-income women are routinely denied access to their data. There is no observation about how several defective units led to unwanted pregnancies in societies where abortion was already considered both a crime and a sin. Most glaringly, the exhibition offers no comment on the extraordinary setbacks in the basic human right of bodily autonomy that allowed such a product to even exist.

¡Hubla!'s ignoring of the negative aspects of Oníria is extensively documented as well: director Heitor Fontana has dismissed criticism towards the project in numerous instances. By presenting this piece of smart jewellery as ¡Hubla!'s first, iconic success story without further context, the exhibition silences the stories of those who were harmed by the system enforced by this product, reinforcing ¡Hubla!'s own narrative. We believe, however, that offering a critical perspective on the designer's role in the establishment of what was, ultimately, a perverse system of surveillance of gendered (and racialized) bodies masquerading as a fertility management tool should be a primary goal of such an exhibition.

Design and the Domestication of Difference:
The Case of 'Ruídografías'

Another strong presence in the exhibition is the series of short-term projects undertaken in the largest occupations in Latin America, particularly in the Southern Cone—Chile, Argentina, Uruguay—plus Brazil. Due to gentrification and the extinction of social housing programmes, displaced and evicted families occupied a good number of abandoned industrial parks, allotments, and buildings in these countries. Many of these occupations lasted less than a month due to media pressure and forced evictions, but several persisted amongst waves of mistrust, hate speech, and segregation, led by 'neighbourhood watches', self-proclaimed 'moral vigilantes' and most of Latin American mass media. The legality of these occupations was the subject of long debates in the media, and online sharing of information about the struggles of the occupations themselves was scarce, but nevertheless showed a side of the story that was largely ignored by corporate media outlets. It is in this delicate context that the Hub, in close collaboration with city councils and urban planning departments, undertook a series of design-driven participatory projects aiming to 'improve communication and integrate the occupations into the neighbourhoods.' Among them is the week-long, multi-city participatory design workshop 'Ruídografías' (roughly translated as 'noiseographics'). The processes and outcomes of these workshops were crucial to the elaboration of contemporary noise-abatement laws in the continent, e.g. 'Lei do Silêncio Inteligente (Decree 1035/22)' (Smart Silence Enforcement Law) in Brazil, or 'Las Normas Inteligentes de Emisión de Ruidos Molestos' (Smart Noise-Abatement Bill)—'DTO-1038-x, AR1041' in Chile and Argentina, respectively. The artefacts exhibited also showcase the methodology used by ¡Hubla! to develop these projects: engaging with the occupations towards developing playful devices for mapping out their own sonic environments, in order to educate the inhabitants over acoustic disturbance, and thus develop 'better listening' practices. These devices recorded overhead soundscapes—which were later used for frequency band sorting and measurement—,

Luiza Prado de O. Martins & Pedro J. S. Vieira de Oliveira

or discrete sounds of the occupations, of specific interest to the lawmakers, in order to feed an ever-growing database of 'undesirable' or 'annoying' acoustic events. These mappings led to the posterior development of 'smart' solutions for muffling or even cancelling out frequency bands, or eliminating certain sounds by using active-noise cancellation techniques and urban furniture.

This section of the exhibition features two of these devices, stemming from different instalments of the workshop, as well as one of the many maps that were generated from these sessions. The first object is a small crimson-and-black kite, which would look ordinary if it weren't for the two piezo microphones, one at the top and the other at the bottom front, connected to a Wi-Fi module glued to the back of the kite.[5] According to the descriptive text for this object, kites like these were built collectively at the beginning of the week, engaging kids, volunteers, and designers from the Hub in an activity which sought to 'bridge traditional forms of play and toy-making with contemporary technologies such as smart sensors, recorders, and other forms of augmented interaction.' Kids were taught how to attach and connect microphones and sensors to the kites in a way that would not disrupt its ability to fly and perform acrobatics in the air. They were also briefly instructed about how the electronic devices in the kite worked, as well as to specific things they should look for when flying the device around, e.g., busy places, spots where music was being played, or any other kind of assembly within the occupation. The kites were flown every day for the entire week and in different parts of the occupations, recording not only overhead soundscapes with the microphones but also collecting other data points such as timestamps, weather data, and flight trajectory. These could be collectively monitored in real time by

5

Early prototype for the kites that would be later built by kids during the workshop.

designers and participants alike, in a playful and educational activity which is documented and exhibited alongside the objects.

There is no information as to whom this kite originally belonged, perhaps in order to protect the identity of the person—by the time still underage—, given the tragic demise of that occupation only a few years after this workshop took place in Brazil. Nevertheless, the reports that follow this particular kite aim to show the success of this simple device, and the visitor is offered the opportunity to listen to a few of these raw recordings. In them, sound events are faint and barely recognizable (there is a lot of wind which was later filtered out by the sound designers), but nevertheless an interesting shift in character of sound is immediately perceptible, when one follows the map together with the recordings moving to the higher parts of the occupation. The overall soundscape seems less populated with sub-bass frequencies (45–200Hz); music is less prominent, giving way to often shouted conversations, multiple fireworks, motorbikes, and the occasional gunshot. These long soundscapes (the shortest clocks at sixteen minutes and fifty-eight seconds) were later taken back to ¡Hubla! and their frequency band predominances were turned into data visualization sculptures[6]—one of which is also available at the exhibition.

The second object from the set belonging to the workshop is a metallic-green earbud.[7] It was originally a *pair* of 'smart binaural microphones', but according to the description of this object, the pair was a one-off device for the event carried out in Greater Valparaiso in Chile, and one of the pieces was unfortunately lost by the participant who wore them. This is a very curious piece, insofar it is a high-end product which was not developed *within* the workshop but rather assembled by ¡Hubla! beforehand, exclusively to be employed in these

6

Data visualization sculpture of the mapped frequency bands at the occupation in Brazil. The larger the indent on the map, the lower the frequency; the deeper, the louder. Two layers are exhibited: one for sub-bass and bass frequencies, and the other for mid-range frequencies.

7

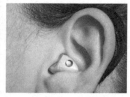

Binaural earbud, similar to the ones used in the workshop.

Luiza Prado de O. Martins & Pedro J. S. Vieira de Oliveira

sessions—hence the top-end technology it makes use of. Simply described, this is a set of discreet wireless binaural microphones with active-noise cancellation headphones—technologies which were available at the time but not exactly state-of-the-art.[8] It also isolates the wearer from external sounds and constrains listening to the experience of the microphones, therefore allowing for a direct experience with what is being heard and recorded. But differently from most technologies for binaural recordings back then, what is remarkable here is the possibility for the wearer to 'zoom into' certain sounds by adjusting the microphone's sensibility to certain frequencies in real time over a smartphone app. The application's interface, also shown in the exhibition, does not require any prior knowledge in sound design, but instead calls the listener's attention to possible 'points of interest' nearby, and asks the wearer whether or not to zoom into those points.

The ¡Hubla! team deployed the earbuds as part of a 'cultural probe' in the occupation, and the device was in use for the entire week by the same person—Pachi Sanhueza, a 54-year old *humitas* seller.[9] The choice for this particular person, according to the exhibition catalogue, was due to the fact she '[was] native to the occupation, knew everybody, and walked all around it as part of her daily job', and as such could access all parts of the occupation thus providing 'varying and comprehensive data from the same place at different days, with little to no intrusion in the soundscape'. Sanhueza was instructed to perform a routine of eavesdropping on her surroundings and selecting, by means of tuning the microphones in and out of conversations and events which she found more interesting. Curiously enough, Pachi's own voice is seldom heard in the recordings, except for her call-and-response selling refrain. Hence, in the listening post one peeks onto an

8
Binaural microphones are stereo microphones split in two separate devices which, due to their placement on the ears of the recordist, capture a stereo image of the soundscape which is slightly delayed from one side to the other (depending on the direction the sound comes from), thus mimicking almost precisely how a human being hears.

9
The Chilean variation of tamale, a popular food in Latin American.

entire universe of dripping faucets, text-messaging apps, muffled music, motorbike horns, as well as heated, long discussions on subjects ranging from football to women, business to telenovelas, and, not surprisingly, politics.

Together, these objects show a comprehensive effort on acquiring as much sound-based data as possible from these occupations: overhead soundscapes, long soundwalks, and a taxonomy of acoustic events that are unique, discrete, and particular of the places they stem from. However, lacking both in the catalogue as well as in the exhibition itself is a discussion around the ethics of sourcing members of the occupations to mine data for the elaboration of policies that tended to benefit the neighbourhoods near the occupations, rather than the occupations themselves. The kites project, for instance, sparked controversy as to the nature and content of the recordings it provided the designers and policy makers with. Also missing in the exhibition is a mention of the backlash against the presence of the Hub in the occupation, coming both from local crime organizations—often resorting to violent acts within the occupation—and community activists, in a rare occasion in which their efforts, usually directed against one another, were slightly in unison. Tracing back the locations where the kites were deployed shows us an interesting pattern of meetings and gatherings of the occupation leaders, as well as to residences of occupation activists and leaders which were involved in the (unfortunately failed) political negotiations against the forced eviction. This is, as one would expect, also omitted from the curatorial statement. Similarly, in Chile the earbuds were met with mistrust by most members of the occupation, and many of Sanhueza's recordings are cut at the exact moment she identifies a threat, or when someone might be approaching her to ask what

Luiza Prado de O. Martins & Pedro J. S. Vieira de Oliveira

she is actually doing. We cannot know with certainty which of her recordings were considered intrusive and unwanted by the occupation itself; nevertheless, subjecting a member of the occupation to the risk of being perceived as an 'assimilated body' by their fellow neighbours, and as such an 'agent' for the status quo—as discussed many times in the history of that particular occupation in Greater Valparaiso—is an irresponsible act that is never discussed or mentioned in the exhibition's documents.

'Ruídografías' was, of course, not the only measure taken by the councils to force the occupations and their leaders to abide to the cities' own terms. Other initiatives attempted to 'embellish' the occupations' architecture, or offered ready-made solutions to urban planning that only created new and bigger problems, instead of addressing them. In that sense, the collection of sounds portrays the recordists' own realities and preferences; their idiosyncrasies and often conflicting mechanisms of dealing with the fine lines between noise and sound, which differ significantly from the 'better listening practices' the project ultimately wanted to achieve. In one of the sound snippets available at the listening post, one can clearly hear the beating of pots and pans against countless barking dogs, while at the same time a distant voice yells for someone to lower the volume of music, to which the person laughingly complies. An *impromptu* interviewee reports the negotiation between perceptions of loud and quiet as 'a matter of respect, not law', because loud sounds may represent both 'joyful and tense times' within the occupation. However, the use of the data collected in these sound snippets—frequency maps, discrete sounds, et cetera—to develop specific devices, be they objects or policies and abatement laws, ended up confining the occupations to a state of non-existence in the soundscape through a process of *silencing by design*. The topography of noise levels and frequencies also demonstrates how 'smart frequency mappings' were more enforced in the occupations in contrast to other neighbourhoods in the studied cities. In other words, their voices and sounds were wiped out of the urban acoustic fabric under a discourse of 'integration' through erasure of (sonic) identity, that is, obliterating the sonic character of the occupations in favour of an enforced perception of 'good practices' of listening. This opens enough room for questioning the invisible— or should we say silent?—influence of this project in the actual physical erasure of the occupations them- selves in the following years, sometimes quite tragically, as was the case in Brazil.

If Not Tomorrow, Then Today

The objects analysed in this review do not, of course, provide an exhaustive representation of ¡Hubla!'s work. They do, however, highlight one of the most problem- atic facets of this brand of social innovation design: a strategically shallow understanding of social inequality, coupled with an tendency to partner with those directly responsible for fostering inequality in the first place. This unwillingness to critically examine design's role in the enforcement of discriminatory systems is not fortuitous, nor unintentional; rather, it derives from the perception of design as an activity (and field of study) that adapts to the problems faced by society, instead of actively questioning why these problems exist, or which power dynamics make them exist in the first place.

The uncritical celebration of this approach to de- sign in the exhibition begs for a reflection: what could have been done differently? Counter-hegemonic

Luiza Prado de O. Martins & Pedro J. S. Vieira de Oliveira

approaches have, unfortunately, long been either dismissed or divested of substance in the field of design research. An epistemological shift is but a slow endeavour; even more so in an environment trained to be brutally biased against ways of thinking that aim to shift power imbalances between privileged and underprivileged, researcher subject and object of research. Attempts to effectively redirect what design could in fact do are successively stifled, commodified as art objects, and misappropriated by narratives of tech-driven utopian futurologies or design contests. Instead of focusing on design's ability to reconfigure ontologies, socially-oriented design waits for a problem to be created in order to develop a way to live with it. This is clear, for instance, with the resurgence of conservatism not only in Latin America but all over the world: instead of designing non-complying artefacts that would expose the flaws and setbacks of the increasing policing of (gendered and racialized) bodies, designers direct their efforts towards a notion of 'preferability' already prefigured into the objects by the morals and values of this very conservative mentality.

By the time ¡Hubla! came into existence, the biggest challenge in Latin America was to avoid losing the minor advances in human rights conquered since the mid-twentieth century. Instead, massive investments were made in the technological development of new products, devices, and systems so as to make the process of losing rights feel all too natural—a domestication of difference to accommodate for a normative way of being that re-enacts the past in the present. Radicalism was confined only to the superficial layers of political action, and understood as that which demanded society to *transcend* politics, instead of using confrontation *as* politics. This way of thinking fostered the erasure of transformative actions in favour of adaptive ones. Transcendence is, after all, just another word for the enactment of privilege.

Little has changed since then, unfortunately, despite what this collection of objects intends to portray. Showcasing and exhibiting these products and prototypes narrates a story of *what could have been, not of what actually happened.* This story is, yet again, told by a perspective that downplays the direct social impact of these designs, in favour of a fictional tale where technological development spontaneously begets social development—a mentality present in Latin America since the 1970s. In truth, 'social', 'sustainable', or 'empathic' design still define those who are entitled to determine the future, and those who are condemned to enact it. These are but mere examples of designing the surface layers in order to cover up [for] the deep social, economic, and political holes caused by design itself. To prevent the policing of bodies—through, among other outlets, the management and control of fertility, or of voices and sounds, as exemplified here—is perhaps the most enduring of challenges; one that does not only pertain to design, but needs it no less. What has constantly been lying ahead for Latin America, in reality, is that which always lurks at the corner of the eye, and it was always there but never quite reachable by design: not development, not sustainability, but emancipation.

Luiza Prado de O. Martins & Pedro J. S. Vieira de Oliveira

NOT DEVELOPMENT

NOT SUSTAINABILITY

BUT EMAN-
CIPATION

Responsible Objects, Utopian Desires
A Two-Sided Monologue on the Future of Design

Marjanne van Helvert

ACTIVIST   It seems like designers have always been actively involved in socially committed design projects, and have often criticized and analysed the achievements and shortcomings of their discipline. Social design and even sustainable design are not some new hype after all, but form a long-standing part of design history, with many celebrated and influential designers acting as passionate advocates for a more socially and environmentally responsible design discipline.

SCEPTIC   So if all these famous designers have been dedicating themselves to social design for the past century and a half, then why are we stuck in this hopeless situation where we hear reports of our impending doom from all sides? Climate change is now unstoppable and already making an impact on the livelihood of the poorest communities of the world. Sea levels are definitely rising. Fossil fuels are on the verge of depletion, as well as causing endless wars and environmental pollution. Biodiversity is declining at an unprecedented rate and we don't even know yet what that will mean for the food chain. The gap between the rich and the poor is widening in many countries, with neo-liberal economics having ended the opposite trend of growing equality. The global number of refugees is at its highest since the Second World War. Climate change will only add to the need for migration in the coming century, yet the world's richest countries are entrenching themselves behind right-wing politics and border fences trying to keep immigrants out, while ignoring and aggravating the present and future

Marjanne van Helvert

causes of migration. It seems like these problems are too big and too complex to solve, and designers have made no difference in them at all.

A But a lot of things have also changed for the better, of course.[1] The average human being is healthier and grows older than ever before, and extreme poverty has been declining steadily worldwide. More people have access to education and the majority of countries in the world are democracies now. There has been a lot of successful environmental legislation, saving many animal species and their habitats from extinction and destruction, and the world's forests actually seem to be recovering after centuries of decline.

1
The website Our World In Data, a project by University of Oxford economist Max Roser, is dedicated to presenting empirical data on social and economic history, in order to provide a more optimistic view on long term developments than we usually see in the media. Its research and visualizations are available under a creative commons licence, and its tools are open source. www.ourworldin-data.org.

S Still, how have designers been involved in any of these improvements? Aren't they mostly caused by social and political change, and by economic prosperity? How much influence do designers really have? With the now widespread use of the concept of 'design thinking', designers are attributed special problem solving skills that supposedly are applicable to 'wicked problems' in any field or discipline, also outside of the traditional design arena. It is an abstract promise of universal creativity, simplifying the ambiguous reality to fit convenient and workable answers, and averting our eyes from the fact that many problems are political and are rooted in complex moral decisions from the past and the present.

A   Big responsibilities are assigned to the design discipline when it is presented as a harbinger of positive change,[2] but it seems less eager to take on accountability for harmful practices and traditions, such as already named by Vance Packard and Victor Papanek, mid-twentieth century. If design is considered this influential in our world and in our future, it should also be accountable for its mistakes. These debates have taken place at various points in history, and we should keep having them.

S   Yet it is still a field that is largely dominated by a global elite that suffers from racist, sexist and many other exclusionary traditions. Some ideas in what we now call social design are rooted in colonial thinking, which favours western practices over local and vernacular ones.

A   That is why it is so important that designers are aware of the complexities of their position as designated or self-defined problem solvers. It is often implied that the act of design is free of ideology and political intent, when it is simply put forward as a successful, pragmatic method for problem solving.[3] But when design is not also a critical activity, it is responsible for reaffirming and reproducing the status quo. If design is going to play a broader role in society, and it is of course already involved even in the most mundane aspects of daily life, it would be well served by a more modest type of responsibility and accountability.

2
Design writers such as Tony Fry, Alastair Fuad-Luke, Victor Margolin and many others have emphasized the importance of design in changing our future.

3
An interesting example of this is the 'Refugee Challenge' initiated by the Dutch design conference 'What Design Can Do', in collaboration with UNHCR and the IKEA Foundation. It presented the arrival of Syrian refugees in Europe as the subject of a design contest, asking designers to come up with creative solutions in several categories ranging from shelter to intercultural communication. By ignoring the ambiguous ideologies and policies behind the precarious status of the refugee and immigrant in Europe, the 'Challenge' silently supported these, asked designers to do so too, and to only look for solutions to the symptoms of these much larges issues. www.whatdesigncando.com/challenge. Some of the debate that took place in reaction to this contest can be followed here: www.archined.nl/2016/05/wdcd-refugee-challenge and here: www.dezeen.com/2016/04/21/ruben-pater-opinion-what-design-can-do-refugee-crisis-problematic-design.

Marjanne van Helvert

S   A call for modesty and responsibility; that is not going to be a popular proposal in a community that thrives on spectacle.

A   Sure, spectacle is spectacular. But so is modesty, and it has an equally impressive history in design. Many designers in this book, from Margarete Schütte-Lihotzky to Victor Papanek, have considered the importance of modesty and accountability in their work. It is a central value of functionalist design aesthetics as well, and it also appears in that classic Modernist dictum 'less is more'. But this call for modesty, responsibility, and accountability is really about designers considering the ideological ambiguity of their practice, and the political impact of their decisions. In the last thirty to forty years, idealism, ideology, and political activism have quite successfully been represented as things of the past, things that block economic progress, while neoliberal ideology itself, implicitly and unnamed, has been put forward as the only way to human progress.[4] The environmental movement, for example, has only recently started to detach itself from the one-sided association with left-wing hippies and tree huggers, as climate change and resource depletion are becoming realities for the corporate world as well. The western design discipline has evolved along with dominant ideologies through history, going from producing purely elitist luxury until the early twentieth century, to offering a socialist tool for emancipation in the first half of the twentieth century, to increasingly driving consumer society as the century progressed. Much of the design world is now so immersed in the

4
British prime minister Margaret Thatcher famously used the slogan 'There Is No Alternative' (TINA) to promote the idea that global free market capitalism is the only possible system for human development.

latter that socially committed design projects are cast as deviations, as something extra to what design normally does, while for quite some time in history they have been a central focus of the discipline. Perhaps we shouldn't regard social design as a separate category, but evaluate all design according to its social responsibility again. That is why it is important that designers are aware of the history of their profession, and of the theories, criticism, and debates that have been put forth over time, so we can see that present-day challenges are not new and have been met with in various ways in the past

> S   The gap between the design practice and design history and theory is pretty big. Designers don't read books!

A   That is just a stereotype.

> S   But history in general is not something that designers particularly want to be associated with. They are more interested in the future, in new technologies and opportunities. When you look too much at history, you run the risk of idealizing it and becoming nostalgic for a time that has in fact never existed. You can see this in the romantic idealism of the Arts & Crafts movement and also of the counterculture movement and the hippies. They glorified the handicrafts, the countryside, pre-industrial production, and even pre-industrial aesthetics, and thought they offered an alternative to the wasteful industrial and mass production of goods. In both cases these movements were caught up with by technology and consumerism.

Marjanne van Helvert

A   Yet today again many designers work with traditional and pre-industrial crafts and techniques, with natural materials, small-scale and local production, collaborative design methods and other 'old-fashioned' practices, especially in areas of social and sustainable design. They often combine old traditions with new technologies to adapt sustainable concepts to current demands and circumstances. Things such as wind power and hydropower are essentially ancient ideas, but they are becoming relevant again as they fulfil contemporary demands. The same is true for natural, renewable materials and fuels. These concepts never really disappeared and are an attractive and fertile ground for new experiments and positive stories, because they come from a time when the impact of humans on their environment was not as prominent and irreversible as it seems today. They deal with resources that can be regrown and replenished within a foreseeable amount of time. In the same vein, local and small-scale production gives designers the opportunity to control more aspects of the production process and thereby reduce harmful practices of the industry. This is a way to take responsibility for more than just the literal design part of the job, and to see design as a broad discipline with consequences in resource extraction, labour conditions, production processes, consumption patterns, energy and material efficiency, waste, and pollution.

S   Not everyone believes these practices are viable on the scale of the current and future human population. Especially not those that sit on the other side of the spectrum, who believe in technology as the answer to our problems: the techno-utopians. Techno-optimism is an equally romantic starting point, though. Technology has been glorified many times in the history of design as well, notably by the Modernists, Buckminster Fuller, and the Anti-Designers for example. But has it brought us the answers we were looking for? Hasn't technological progress been one of the main instigators of pollution, waste, inhuman working conditions, et cetera? When is that magical moment going to occur, when all of our technological knowledge will be devoted to solving some of these issues? If there is no profitable outcome in financial terms, no one seems to want to invest in technology that could improve social conditions or our natural environment.

A   Eventually though, solving our biggest environmental issues will become profitable, because our comfort, if not our very survival, will come to depend on it.

S   That will only happen once a lot of irreversible damage is done. It is also bad news for the poorest and most vulnerable communities and individuals in the world, who will most likely not be able to benefit equally from these future solutions, as for-profit technological solutions are only available to those who have the means to acquire them.

A   Which is why people are looking for ways to change this scenario. Many designers are reconsidering that secondary act of designing

Marjanne van Helvert

that they are responsible for, when a design leaves the realm of ideas and enters the real world, through the machines and hands of producers, through the means of transportation by which it travels the world, by the way in which it is used, and the way in which it is eventually discarded. All of these steps and the moral choices involved in them are part of the design, and all of them together decide its influence on the world and its concurrent designing of experiences, of culture, nature, and eventually the future. Both new technologies and 'old' sustainable methods and resources are needed in the process of dealing with environmental challenges and dealing with them fairly. Only sustainable design is social design; and only a social future is sustainable.

S   Who is going to believe another design book ending with a call for 'change'?

A   This is not a call for change, this is a call for continuity. Let's continue to be utopian like William Morris, and revolutionary like the teachers and students at Bauhaus and VKhUTEMAS. Let's be uncompromising like Margarete Schütte-Lihotzky, and perfect a socialist experiment like the Utility Scheme. We should be techno-optimists like Buckminster Fuller, Do-It-Yourselvers like the hippies, *and* romanticize craftsmanship. We have to become Radical Anti-Designers as well as humanitarian ones. We should all devote at least 10% of our work to a social cause, like Victor Papanek suggested, and take 100% responsibility. Let's take the moral high ground, be spectacularly modest, become politically correct, think and talk about obsolescence, about queer theory, about vernacular design, the next industrial revolution, about privilege and emancipation. Pick one, or try them all. Together they spell progress, which is the only way forward.

This conversation repeatedly took place inside my head while working on this book. It is a conversation between the activist and the sceptic in me, discussing finding inspiration in design history, the future of design as a social kind of design, ideals and ideology, technology and romanticism, speculations, criticism, and responsibility. The cynical rationale of the sceptic sometimes seems hard to defeat, but the fact that this book has made it out of its slipstream proves that the activist must have secretly won again.

Contributors

Editor / Author

MARJANNE VAN HELVERT is a designer and theorist. She received a MA cum laude in Cultural Studies from the Radboud Universiteit Nijmegen in 2007, and a BDes in Textile Design from the Rietveld Academie Amsterdam in 2013. She explores the dynamics between theory and practice of design, and her main fields of interest are the relation between ethics and aesthetics, DIY practices, gender politics, utopia and dystopia. She is currently working on *Dirty Clothes*, a recycled DIY clothing label and magazine. Other projects include the ongoing curtain landscape project, and her manifesto *Dirty Design* (2013). Marjanne lives and works in Amsterdam, the Netherlands.

Authors

ANDREA BANDONI is a designer and teacher, and she was one of the founders of the Fab Lab Brasil Network. She holds a Master in Conceptual Design from the Design Academy Eindhoven, the Netherlands, and has graduated in architecture at FAU USP, Brazil. Her main projects involve objects, interiors and exhibition design. Sustainability and the balance between nature and technology are important themes in her work. Recent projects include the Seringueira [Rubber Tree] Series (2015), and *Objetos da Floresta / Objects of the Forest* (2012). Andrea lives and works in São Paulo, Brazil.

ECE CANLI is a design researcher and performance artist. She holds a B.Sc. in Industrial Product Design from Istanbul Technical University, Turkey, and a MFA in Interdisciplinary Studies/Experience Design from Konstfack University College of Arts, Crafts and Design, Sweden. She is currently a PhD candidate in the Design programme at the University of Porto, Portugal, funded by FCT, where she studies the intersection between queer theory and design practice while exploring possible ways of deconstructing and interrupting oppressive material regimes imposed on gendered, sexualized and marginalized bodies. Her research tools include artefacts, texts, sound and voice. Her recent works are *Silence of Academy/Academy of Silence* (2012), *Queering Design* (2014) and *MANHOLE* (2016).

ALISON J. CLARKE is chair of design history, and director of the Papanek Foundation at the University of Applied Arts Vienna. A trained social anthropologist (PhD, UCL) and historian (V&A/RCA, London), she has published and lectured widely in the field of design and anthropology. She is co-founder and co-editor of *Home Cultures: Journal of Design, Architecture and Domestic Space*, author of *Design Anthropology: Object Cultures in Transition* (2017), and co-editor (with Elana Shapira) of *Émigré Cultures in Design and Architecture* (2017). A regular contributor to media, including the award-winning BBC series *The Genius of Design*, Alison is presently working on an MIT monograph exploring the historical origins of 1960s and 70s design activism.

DESIGNERS DON'T

ÉVA FORGÁCS is an art historian, critic, essayist, and curator, whose fields of research and interest are Modernism and contemporary art and culture. She holds a PhD in Art History from the Hungarian Academy of Sciences, and has been teaching at the Art Center College of Design in Pasadena, California, since 1994. Her publications include *Between Worlds. A Sourcebook of Central European Avant-Gardes 1910–1930* (ed. with T.O. Benson) (The MIT Press, 2002), and *The Bauhaus Idea and Bauhaus Politics* (CEU Press, 1995).

SUSAN R. HENDERSON is Professor of Architectural History at the School of Architecture, Syracuse University, Syracuse, New York. Her publications range from early-twentieth-century esotericism to social architecture during the Weimar Republic in Germany, to studies of hybrid conditions in Islamic architecture. Her most recent book is *Building Culture: Ernst May and the New Frankfurt Initiative, 1926–1932* (Peter Lang, 2013). Other recent publications can be found in *Planning Perspectives*, the *Journal of the Society of Architectural Historians* and *Architectural Review,* as well as book chapters in Renate Hejduk and Jim Williamson's *The Religion Imagination and Modern Architecture* and Barbara Miller Lane's *Housing and Dwelling*.

ED VAN HINTE is a writer, editor, curator, and teacher. He graduated in Industrial Design and Engineering at the University of Technology in Delft. A major theme in his work is the consequences of diminishing material production and consumption by product lifespan extension and mass reduction. His books include *Products That Last: Product Design for Circular Business Models* (co-authored with Conny Bakker, Marcel den Hollander, Yvo Zijlstra) (Marcel den Hollander, 2014), *Lightness: The Inevitable Renaissance of Minimum*

Energy Structures (with Adriaan Beukers) (010 Publishers, 1998), and *Eternally Yours: Visions on Product Endurance* (010 Publishers, 1997).

ELIZABETH CAROLYN MILLER is Professor of English at the University of California, Davis. She received a PhD from the University of Wisconsin, Madison in 2003, and her scholarly interests include nineteenth- and early-twentieth-century British literature and culture, gender studies, film and visuality, print culture, media studies, eco-criticism, and radical politics. Recent publications are *Slow Print: Literary Radicalism and Late Victorian Print Culture* (Stanford University Press, 2013), and *Framed: The New Woman Criminal in British Culture at the Fin de Siècle* (University of Michigan Press, 2008). She is currently working on a book about ecology and capital in nineteenth-century British literature and culture.

LUIZA PRADO DE O. MARTINS & PEDRO J. S. VIEIRA DE OLIVEIRA are both currently PhD candidates in Design Research at the Universität der Künste Berlin. Luiza holds a Bachelor degree in Design from PUC, Rio de Janeiro, and Pedro studied Graphic Design at UNESP Bauru, São Paulo. They both received their MA in Digital Media from the Hochschule für Künste, Bremen. Working collaboratively as 'A Parede', the premise of their research is to use design as a method for political literacy, and to explore the accountability of material practices in securing and perpetuating issues rooted in coloniality such as gender and sonic violence. Recent projects include *Brasil, July 2038* (2014), and *Cheat-Sheet for a Non (or Less) Colonialist Speculative Design* (2014).

Publishers

VALIZ is an international independent publisher and addresses critical developments in contemporary art, theory, critique, design, typography and urban culture. Our books offer reflection and interdisciplinary inspiration, and often establish a connection between cultural disciplines and socio-economic and political questions. We publish these books out of our commitment to their content, to artistic and social issues and to the artists, designers and authors.
www.valiz.nl

UEBERSCHWARZ is a new publishing venture that deals with the design and aesthetics of the built and manufactured environment throughout the twentieth century to the present, analysed from a diverse range of perspectives by professionals and new emerging voices. Ueberschwarz reaches out to the specialist and non-specialist alike, through the publication of books and its quarterly journal, *Unterweiss*.
www.ueberschwarz.com

Bibliography

Introduction

Bruinsma, Max, and Ida van Zijl, eds. *Design for the Good Society: Utrecht Manifest, 2005–2015*. Rotterdam: nai010, 2015.

Buchanan, Richard. 'Wicked Problems in Design Thinking'. *Design Issues* 8, no. 2 (Spring 1992), pp. 5–21.

'Design Ecologies. Nordes 2015'. nordes.org/nordes2015 (accessed 26 July 2016).

Dunne, Anthony, and Fiona Raby. *Design Noir: The Secret Life of Electronic Objects*. Basel, Boston and Berlin: Birkhäuser 2001.

Ericson, Magnus, and Ramia Mazé, eds. *Design Act: Socially and Politically Engaged Design Today: Critical Roles and Emerging Tactics*. Stockholm: Iaspis, and Berlin: Sternberg Press, 2011.

Fuad-Luke, Alastair. *Design Activism: Beautiful Strangeness for a Sustainable World*. London: Earthscan, 2009.

Forty, Adrian. *Objects of Desire: Design and Society 1750–1980*. London: Thames & Hudson, 1986.

Morozov, Evgeny. 'Making It'. *The New Yorker* 13 January 2014. www.new yorker.com/magazine/2014/01/13/making-it-2 (accessed 12 May 2016).

'"Project Bauhaus": 5 Inquiries into an Unfinished Idea'. projekt-bauhaus. de/en (accessed 26 July 2016).

Van der Zwaag, Anne, ed. *Looks Good, Feels Good, Is Good: How Social Design Changes Our World*. Eindhoven: Lecturis, 2014.

William Morris

Adamson, Glenn. *Industrial Strength Design: How Brooks Stevens Shaped Your World*. Boston: MIT Press, 2003.

Altick, Richard. *The English Common Reader: A Social History of the Mass Reading Public, 1800–1900*. 2nd ed. Columbus: Ohio State University Press, 1998.

Barringer, Tim. *Men at Work: Art and Labour in Victorian Britain*. New Haven: Yale University Press, 2005.

Cave, Roderick. *Fine Printing and Private Presses*. London: British Library, 2001.

Clair, Colin. *A History of Printing in Britain*. London: Cassell, 1965.

Dreyfus, John. 'William Morris: Typographer'. In *William Morris and the Art of the Book*, pp. 71-96. New York: Pierpont Morgan Library, 1976.

Eisenstein, Elizabeth. *The Printing Revolution in Early Modern Europe*, 2nd ed. Cambridge: Cambridge University Press, 2005.

Frow, Edmund, and Ruth Edmund. *William Morris in Manchester and Salford.* Salford: Working Class Movement Library, 1996.

Genz, Marcella D. *A History of the Eragny Press.* London: Oak Knoll, 2004

—. *In Fine Print: William Morris as a Book Designer.* London: London Borough of Waltham Forest, Libraries and Arts Department, 1976.

Marx, Karl, and Friedrich Engels. *The Communist Manifesto,* 1848. In Marx, *Selected Writings,* edited by Lawrence H. Simon, pp. 157–86. Indianapolis: Hackett, 1994.

Mitchell, Sally. *Daily Life in Victorian England.* Westport: Greenwood, 1996.

Morris, William. *The Ideal Book: Essays and Lectures on the Arts of the Book,* edited by William S. Peterson, pp. 67–73. Berkeley: University of California Press, 1982.

—. *Political Writings of William Morris,* edited by A.L. Morton. New York: International Publishers, 1973.

—. *Three Works By William Morris,* edited by A.L. Morton. New York: International Publishers, 1986.

—. *Socialist Diary,* edited by Florence Boos. Iowa City: Windhover Press, 1981.

—. *The Story of the Glittering Plain or the Land of Living Men,* facsimile of the 1894 Kelmscott edition. New York: Dover, 1987.

—. *News from Nowhere* (1890), edited by Stephen Arata. Peterborough: Broadview, 2003.

Peterson, William S. *The Kelmscott Press: A History of William Morris's Typographical Adventure.* Oxford: Clarendon, 1991.

Slade, Giles. *Made to Break: Technology and Obsolescence in America.* Cambridge: Harvard University Press, 2006.

Stansky, Peter. *Redesigning the World: William Morris, the 1880s, and the Arts and Crafts.* Princeton: Princeton University Press, 1985, rpt. Palo Alto: Society for the Promotion of Science and Scholarship, 1996.

Thompson, E.P. *William Morris: Romantic to Revolutionary.* New York: Pantheon, 1955.

Thompson, Michael. *Rubbish Theory: The Creation and Destruction of Value.* Oxford: Oxford University Press, 1979.

Veblen, Thorstein. *Theory of the Leisure Class,* 1899. Harmondsworth, Middlesex: Penguin, 1979.

A Political Education – Bauhaus, VKhUTEMAS

Abramova, Alina. 'Vchutemas—Vchutein (1918–1930)'. *Rassegna sovietica* 18, no. 4 (1968), pp. 128–42.

Droste, Magdalene, *Bauhaus. Cologne: Taschen, 2006.*

Ehrenburg, Ilya. *Emberek, évek, életem* [People, years and life]. Translated by János Elbert. Budapest: Gondolat, 1963.

Gray, Camilla. *The Russian Experiment in Art 1863–1922.* London: Thames & Hudson, 1962.

Hüter, Karl-Heinz. *Das Bauhaus in Weimar.* Berlin: Akademie-Verlag, 1976.

Jaeggi, Annemarie. 'Relations between the Bauhaus and the Russian Avant-Garde as Documented in the Collection of the Bauhaus Archive Berlin'. In *Moscow—Berlin: Interchanges and Heritage of the 20th Century*, pp. 154–57. www.icomos.org/risk/2007/pdf/Soviet_Heritage_34_V-4_Jaeggi.pdf.

Khan-Magomedov, Selim. *Georgii Krutikov: The Flying City and Beyond*. Translated by Christina Lodder. Barcelona: Tenov Books, 2015.

Lavrentiev, Alexander. *Varvara Stepanova: The Complete Work*. Cambridge: The MIT Press, 1988.

Lodder, Christina. *Russian Constructivism*. London, New Haven: Yale University Press, 1983.

Taut, Bruno. 'Architektur-Programm' (December 1918). In *Programme und Manifeste zur Architektur des 20. Jahrhunderts*, edited by Ulrich Conrads, pp. 38–40. Berlin: Birkhäuser, 1964.

Wick, Rainer. *Bauhaus Pädagogik*. Cologne: DuMont Buchverlag, 1982.

Margarete Schütte-Lihotzky

'Die Frankfurter Küche war ein Umsturz in den Eigentumsverhältnissen'. *Frankfurter Stadt-Rundschau* 23 January 1997.

Henderson, Susan R. *Building Culture: Ernst May and the Frankfurt Initiative, 1926–1932*. Studies in Modern European History 64. *New York etc.: Peter Lang, 2013*.

Hochhäusl, Sophie. 'From Vienna to Frankfurt inside Core-House Type 7: A History of Scarcity through the Modern Kitchen'. *Architectural Histories* no. 1, November 2013, pp. 1–19.

Lihotzki [sic], Grete. 'Einige über die Einrichtung österreichischer Häuser unter besonderer Berücksichtigung der Siedlungsbauten'. *Schlesisches Heim* no. 8, August 1921, pp. 217–22.

Minoli, Lorenza, et al., eds. *Dalla cucina alla città: Margarete Schütte-Lihotzky*. Milan: FrancoAngeli, 1999.

Noever, Peter, et al., eds. *Margarete Schütte-Lihotzky: Soziale Architektur: Zeitzeugin eines Jahrhunderts*. Vienna: Böhlau Verlag, 1996.

Rukschcio, Burkhardt, and Roland Schachel. *Adolf Loos: Leben und Werk*. Vienna: Residenz, 1982.

Good Design for Everyone

Attfield, Judy, ed. *Utility Reassessed: The Role of Ethics in the Practice of Design*. Manchester: Manchester University Press, 1999.

Brown, Mike. *CC41 Utility Clothing: The Label That Transformed British Fashion*. Sevenoaks: Sabrestorm Publishing, 2014.

Denney, Matthew. 'Utility Furniture and the Myth of Utility 1943–48'. In *Utility Reassessed: The Role of Ethics in the Practice of Design*, edited by Judy Attfield, pp. 110–24. Manchester: Manchester UP, 1999.

Goodbun, Jon, et al., *The Design of Scarcity*. London: Strelka Press, 2014.

Make Do and Mend: Keeping Family and Home Afloat on War Rations. London: Michael O'Mara, 2007.

Massey, Anne, and Paul Micklethwaite. 'Unsustainability: Towards a New Design History with Reference to British Utility'. *Design Philosophy Papers* 7, no. 2 (2009), pp. 123–35.

Pinch, Philip, and Suzanne Reimer. 'Nationalising Local Sustainability: Lessons from the British Wartime Utility Furniture Scheme'. *Geoforum* 65 (24 July 2015), pp. 86–95.

Robinson, Julian. *Fashion in the 40s*. New York: St. Martin's, 1980.

Russell, Gordon. 'What Is Good Design?' *Design* 1 (January 1949), pp. 2–6. www.vads.ac.uk/learning/designingbritain/pdf/crd_2.pdf.

Summers. Julie. *Fashion on the Ration: Style in the Second World War*. London: Profile Books, 2015.

Teijmant, Ineke, and Bart Sorgedrager. *De Verfdoos 1956–2009*. Amsterdam: Lubberhuizen, 2010.

Utility Furniture and Fashion: 1941–1951. London: Geffrye Museum, 1974.

Walford, Jonathan. *Forties Fashion: From Siren Suits to the New Look*. London: Thames & Hudson, 2008.

Design for Consumer Society

DiClerico, Daniel. 'HP Inkjet Printer Lawsuit Reaches $5 Million Settlement'. *Consumer Reports* 17 November 2010. www.consumerreports.org/cro/news/2010/11/hp-inkjet-printer-lawsuit-reaches-5-million-settlement/index.htm (accessed 25 April 2016).

Forty, Adrian. *Objects of Desire*. New York: Pantheon Books, 1986.

London, Bernard. 'Ending the Depression Through Planned Obsolescence'. *Wikimedia*, upload.wikimedia.org/wikipedia/commons/2/27/London_(1932)_Ending_the_depression_through_planned_obsolescence.pdf.

McDonough, William, and Michael Braungart. *Cradle to Cradle: Remaking the Way We Make Things*. New York: North Point Press, 2002.

Miller, A. Edward. 'Hasty Conclusions About Waste'. Review of The Waste Makers. *Journal of Marketing* 25, no. 4 (1961), p. 109–10.

Nader, Ralph. *Unsafe at Any Speed: The Designed-in Dangers of the American Automobile*. New York: Grossman, 1965.

Packard, Vance. *The Hidden Persuaders*. New York: D. McKay, 1957.

—. *The Status Seekers: An Exploration of Class Behavior in America and the Hidden Barriers That Affect You, Your Community, Your Future*. New York: D. McKay, 1959.

—. *The Waste Makers*. London: Longmans, 1960.

Papanek, Victor. *Design for the Real World: Human Ecology and Social Change*. London: Thames & Hudson, 2011.

Slade, Giles. *Made to Break: Technology and Obsolescence in America*. Cambridge: Harvard University Press, 2006,

Stuever, Hank. 'Battery And Assault'. *The Washington Post* 20 December 2003. Also see: www.washingtonpost.com/archive/lifestyle/2003/12/20/battery-and-assault/29056cfd-59d7-4dc7-b12f-cda99203ae6d (accessed 25 April, 2016).

Wiens, Kyle. 'The New MacBook Pro: Unfixable, Unhackable, Untenable'. *Wired* 14 June 2012. www.wired.com/2012/06/opinion-apple-retina-displa (accessed 25 April 2016).

The Buckminster Fuller Mission

'Buckminster Fuller's Dymaxion Car'. www.youtube.com/watch?v=YILZE23EJKs (accessed 1 March 2016).

'Everything I Know' session 01. www.youtube.com/watch?v=o6yaSLipeWg (accessed 1 March 2016).

en.wikipedia.org/wiki/Biphasic_and_polyphasic_sleep

en.wikipedia.org/wiki/Buckminster_Fuller

en.wikipedia.org/wiki/Club_of_Rome

en.wikipedia.org/wiki/Ephemeralization

Lichtenstein, Claude, and Joachim Krausse. *Your Private Sky: R. Buckminster Fuller. The Art of Design Science*. Zürich: Lars Müller Publishers, 1999.

'The World of Buckminster Fuller'. www.youtube.com/watch?v=VFwDABCGr7o (accessed 1 March 2016).

www.quora.com/Can-a-geodesic-dome-over-a-city-work-in-practicality

www.synchronofile.com

The Humanitarian Object – Victor Papanek

Clarke, Alison J. 'Design for Development, ICSID and UNIDO: The Anthropological Turn in 1970s Design'. *Journal of Design History* 29, no. 1 (2016), pp. 43-57.

Clarke, Alison J. 'The Chrome-Plated Marshmallow: The 1960s Consumer Revolution and its Discontents'. In *You Say You Want a Revolution: Records and Rebels 1966–70*. London: V&A, 2016.

Diemer, Ulli. 'How Things Don't Work: Victor Papanek & James Hennessey'. *Seven News* August 1978.

'Gadgets That Don't Work Bother Designer'. *The Victoria Advocate* 30 June 1977.

Isaacs, Ken. 'Review: The Green Imperative: Design for the Real World by Victor Papanek'. *Design Issues* 13, no. 2 (1997), pp. 78-79.

Papanek, Victor. 'Do-It-Yourself Murder: Social and Moral Responsibilities of Design'. *SDO Journal* (1968), p. 26.

—. 'Pop Culture'. *The Raleigh Times* 17 August 1963.

—. *Design for Real World: Human Ecology and Social Change*. New York: Pantheon Books, 1971.

Counterculture and Anti-Design

Abdulla, Danah. 'A Manifesto of Change or Design Imperialism? A Look at the Purpose of the Social Design Practice'. In *A Matter of Design: Making Society through Science and Technology*, edited by Claudio Coletta et al., pp. 245–60. Milan: STS Italia Publishing, 2014. www.stsitalia.org/conferences/STSITALIA_2014/STS_Italia_AMoD_Proceedings_2014.pdf.

Aureli, Pier Vittorio. *The Project of Autonomy: Politics and Architecture Within and Against Capitalism*. New York: Temple Hoyne Buell Center for the Study of American Architecture, 2008.

Bicknell, Julian, and Liz McQuiston. *Design for Need: The Social Contribution of Design: An Anthology of Papers Presented to the Symposium at the Royal College of Art, London, April, 1976*. Oxford: Published for ICSID by Pergamon Press, 1977.

Brand, Stewart, ed. *Whole Earth Catalog: Access to Tools* (Menlo Park, CA: Portola Institute, 1968).

Brand, Stewart. *Whole Earth Discipline: An Eco-pragmatist Manifesto*. New York: Viking, 2009.

Branzi, Andrea. *No-stop City: Archizoom Associati*. Orléans: HYX, 2006.

Brown, Ann. 'Neocolonialism in Design for Development'. *Making Futures Journal* 3 (28 March 2014). www.plymouthart.ac.uk/documents/Brown__Ann.pdf.

Buckminster Fuller, Richard. 'The Designers and the Politicians'. In *Beyond Left and Right: Radical Thought for Our Times*, edited by Richard Kostelanetz, pp. 364–70. New York: William Morrow and Co. Inc., 1968.

Constant Nieuwenhuys. 'New Babylon'. isites.harvard.edu/fs/docs/icb.topic709752.files/WEEK 7/CNieuwenhuis_New Babylon.pdf (accessed 30 April 2016).

Glancey, Jonathan. 'Anti-Matter'. *The Guardian* 31 March 2003. www.theguardian.com/artanddesign/2003/mar/31/architecture.artsfeatures (accessed 4 May 2016).

Hennessey, James, and Victor J. Papanek. *Nomadic Furniture*. New York: Pantheon Books, 1973.

Horvitz, Robert. 'Whole Earth Culture: Exploring Whole Earth'. Whole Earth Catalog. wholeearth.com/history-whole-earth-culture.php (accessed 18 April 2016).

Isaacs, Ken. *How to Build Your Own Living Structures*. New York: Harmony Books, 1974.

Jameson, Fredric. *Postmodernism, Or, The Cultural Logic of Late Capitalism*. Durham: Duke University Press, 1991.

Kahn, Lloyd. 'Domography'. Interview by Julianne Gola and Yukiko Bowman. *Volume* 24 (2010), p. 77.

Kahn, Lloyd. *Domebook 1* and *2*. Los Gatos: Pacific Domes, 1970 and 1971.

Le-Mentzel, Van Bo and Birgit S. Bauer. *Hartz IV Moebel.com: Build More—Buy Less: Konstruieren statt Konsumieren*. Ostfildern: Hatje Cantz, 2012.

Madge, Pauline. 1993. 'Design, Ecology, Technology: A Historiographical

Review'. *Journal of Design History* 6, no. 3 (1993), pp. 149–66. www.jstor.org/stable/1316005.

Mari, Enzo. *Autoprogettazione?* 1974, reprint Mantova: Corraini, 2002.

Papanek, Victor. *Design for the Real World: Human Ecology and Social Change*. London: Thames & Hudson, 2011.

Superstudio. 'Superstudio: Projects and Thoughts'. *Domus* 11 February 2012. www.domusweb.it/en/from-the-archive/2012/02/11/superstudio-projects-and-thoughts.html (accessed 29 April 2016). Originally published in *Domus* 479 (October 1969).

'Superstudio'. Wikipedia. en.wikipedia.org/wiki/Superstudio (accessed 30 April 2016).

www.hipporoller.org

www.littlesun.com

Design History Interrupted – A Queer-Feminist Perspective

Attfield, Judith. 'FORM/female FOLLOWS FUNCTION/male: Feminist Critiques of Design'. In *Design History and the History of Design*, edited by John A. Walker, pp. 199–21. London: Pluto Press, 1989.

Buckley, Cheryl. 'Made in Patriarchy: Toward a Feminist Analysis of Women and Design'. *Design Issues* 3, no. 2 (1986), pp. 3–14.

Canlı, Ece. '[Non]Gendered Desires: Queer Possibilities in Design'. *DESIGNA 2014 Proceedings*, edited by Universidada da Beira Interior et al., p. 277–88 (Colvilhã: UBI, 2015). www.labcom-ifp.ubi.pt/ficheiros/201602151153-designa_2014_proceedings.pdf.

Cockburn, Cynthia, and Susan Ormrod. *Gender and Technology in the Making*. London and Thousand Oaks: Sage, 1993.

Crenshaw, Kimberlé. 'Demarginalizing the Intersection of Race and Sex: A Black Feminist Critique of Antidiscrimination Doctrine, Feminist Theory and Antiracist Politics'. *University of Chicago Legal Forum (PhilPapers)* 140 (1989), pp. 139–67.

De Bretteville, Sheila Levrant. 'A Re-examination of Some Aspects of the Design Arts from the Perspective of a Woman Designer'. *Arts in Society* 11, no. 1 (1974), pp. 114–23.

De Grazia, Victoria, and Ellen Furlough, eds. *The Sex of Things: Gender and Consumption in Historical Perspective*, Berkeley and Los Angeles: University of California Press, 1996.

Ehrenreich, Barbara, and Annette Fuentes. 'Life on the Global Assembly Line'. *Ms. Magazine* 9, no. 7 (January 1981), pp. 52-59.

Goffman, Erving. *Gender Advertisements*. New York: Harper & Row, 1976.

Goodall, Philippa. 'Design and Gender'. *block* 9 (1983), pp. 50–61.

Gorman, Carma. 'Reshaping and Rethinking: Recent Feminist Scholarship on Design and Designers'. *Design Issues* 17, no. 4 (2001), pp. 72–88.

Hill Collins, Patricia. *Black Feminist Thought: Knowledge, Consciousness, and* the Politics of Empowerment. London and New York: Routledge, 2000.

Kazi-Tani, Tiphaine. 'Queer Graphics. The Critical Work of Hélène Mourrier'. In *ENVELOPE 2015: Designing Critical Messages, Plymouth, United Kingdom,* February 2015. halshs.archives-ouvertes.fr/halshs-01120242/document.

Kirkham, Pat, ed. *The Gendered Object.* Manchester: Manchester University Press, 1996.

Maher, Gabriel Ann. 'De__Sign: Revealing the Condition of the Mediated Body'. In *The Virtuous Circle: Design Culture and Experimentation: Proceedings of the Cumulus Conference, June 3–7, Milan,* edited by Luisa Collina, Laura Galluzzo and Anna Meroni, pp. 1051–65. Milan: Unitec, 2015.

Matrix. *Making Space: Women and the Man Made Environment.* London: Pluto Press, 1984.

McQuiston, Liz. *Women in Design: A Contemporary View (London and New York, 1988).*

muf. 'An Invisible Privilege'. In *Altering Practices: Feminist Politics and Poetics of Space,* edited by Doina Petrescu. London and New York: Routledge, 2007.

Nochlin, Linda. 'Why Have There Been No Great Women Artists?' *Art News* 69, no. 9 (January 1971), pp. 22-39, 67-71.

Pathmakers: Women in Art, Craft, and Design, Mid-century and Today Exhibition (New York: National Museum of Women in the Arts, 2016).

Prado de O. Martins, Luiza. 'Pills, Genders and Design: Speculations on Queer Materialities'. 2015. www.academia.edu/24586798/Pills_genders_and_design_Speculations_on_Queer_Materialities.

Scotford, Martha. 'Toward an Expanded View of Women in Graphic Design'. *Visible Language* 28, no. 4 (1994), pp. 367–87.

Sparke, Penny. *As Long as It's Pink: The Sexual Politics of Taste.* London: Pandora and San Francisco: HarperCollins , 1995.

Williamson, Judith. *Decoding Advertisements.* New York: Boyars, 1984.

Women Designers in the USA, 1900–2000: Diversity and Difference, edited by Pat Kirkham. New York: The Bard Graduate Center for Studies in the Decorative Arts, Design and Culture, 2002.

The Digital Age Reaches the Fringes – Fab Lab

Amazon Floating Fab Lab. 2014. amazon.fablat.org/en/fab-flotante-amazonas (accessed 26 April 2016).

Bandoni, Andrea, and Florian Jakober. *Objects of the Forest: Exploring the Amazon through Designer's Eyes.* São Paulo: Andrea Bandoni de Oliveira, 2012. objetosdafloresta.files.wordpress.com/2014/07/objects-of-the-forest-en.pdf.

Boufleur, Rodrigo. 'A Questão da Gambiarra: Formas alternativas de desenvolver artefatos e suas relações com o design de produtos'. Master thesis diss., University of São Paulo, 2006. www.teses.usp.br/teses/disponiveis/16/16134/tde-24042007-150223/pt-br.php.

Büching, Corinne. 'A Universe of Objects'. In *Fab Lab: of Machines, Makers and Inventors*, edited by Julia Walter-Herrmann and Corinne Büching, pp. 106–18. Wetzlar: Transcript, 2013.

Fab Foundation. 'The Fab Charter'. 2015. www.fabfoundation.org/fab-labs/the-fab-charter (accessed 26 April 2016).

Fab Foundation. 'Who/What Qualifies as a Fab Lab?'. 2015. www.fabfoundation.org/fab-labs/fab-lab-criteria (accessed 26 April 2016).

Fonseca, Felipe. *Repair Culture*. 2015. efeefe.no-ip.org/livro/repair-culture (accessed 26 April 2016).

Gershenfeld, Neil. 'How to Make Almost Anything: The Digital Fabrication Revolution'. *Foreign Affairs* 91, no. 6 (November-December 2012), pp. 43–57.

Menotti, Gabriel. '*Gambiarra: the prototyping perspective*'. *Paper presented at the Interactivos?'10: Neighborhood Science workshop, Media Lab Prado – Madrid, June 7–23*. 2010. medialab-prado.es/article/gambiarra.

Neves, Heloisa. 'Maker Innovation: Do Open Design e Fab Labs... às estratégias inspiradas no movimento maker'. PhD diss., University of São Paulo, 2014.

Ozorio de Almeida Meroz, Joana and Rachel Griffin. 'Open Design: A History of the Construction of a Dutch Idea'. In *Pruys Bekaert 2014*, edited by Archined and Designplatform Rotterdam, pp. 27–35. 2014. www.ontwerp-schrijfkunst.org/wp/wp-content/uploads/2013/09/OSK-webpub-secure.pdf (accessed 26 April 2016).

Rawsthorn, Alice. *Hello World: Where Design Meets Life*. London: Penguin Books, 2013.

Troxler, Peter. 'Making the Third Industrial Revolution'. In *Fab Lab: of Machines, Makers and Inventors*, edited by Julia Walter-Herrmann and Corinne Büching, pp. 181–94. Wetzlar: Transcript, 2013.

Walter-Herrmann, Julia, and Corinne Büching. 'Notes on Fab Labs'. In *Fab Lab: Of Machines, Makers and Inventors*, edited by Julia Walter-Herrmann and Corinne Büching, pp. 10–23. Wetzlar: Transcript, 2013.

Zindel, Karin. 'Field Trip to Brazil: Design Lab Brazil: Learning from the Informal'. 2015. master.design.zhdk.ch/news/design-lab-brazil-learning-from-the-informal (accessed 26 April 2016).

Responsible Objects – A Two-Sided Monologue

www.ourworldindata.org
www.archined.nl/2016/05/wdcd-refugee-challenge
www.dezeen.com/2016/04/21/ruben-pater-opinion-what-design-can-do-refugee-crisis-problematic-design
www.whatdesigncando.com/challenge

ONLY SUSTAINABLE DESIGN IS SOCIAL DESIGN, DESIGN IS DESIGN,

ONLY A SOCIAL FUTURE IS SUSTAINABLE

Index

Colophon

Editor: Marjanne van Helvert
Contributors: Andrea Bandoni, Ece Canlı, Alison J.
Clarke, Éva Forgács, Marjanne van Helvert, Susan R.
Henderson, Ed van Hinte, Elizabeth Carolyn Miller, Luiza
Prado de O. Martins & Pedro J. S. Vieira de Oliveira
Image research: Marjanne van Helvert
Copy-editing: Leo Reijnen
Proofreading: Els Brinkman
Index: Elke Stevens

Graphic design: Ruben Pater
Typefaces: Founders Grotesk and
Founder Grotesk text by Kris Sowersby
Typeface of the quotes: custom design by Ruben Pater
Paper inside: Munken Print White 80 grs
Paper cover: Munken Pure 240 grs
Lithography: Ten Brink, Meppel
Printing: Drukkerij Tienkamp, Groningen
Publisher: Astrid Vorstermans, Valiz, Amsterdam;
Stephen Palmer, Ueberschwarz, Melbourne

International distribution
BE/NL/LU: Centraal Boekhuis, www.centraal.boekhuis.nl
GB/IE: Anagram Books, www.anagrambooks.com
Europe (excl GB/IE)/Asia: Idea Books, www.ideabooks.nl
Australia: Perimeter, www.perimeterdistribution.com
USA, Canada, Latin-America: D.A.P., www.artbook.com
Individual orders: www.valiz.nl; info@valiz.nl

This publication was made possible through the
generous support of: the Creative Industries Fund, NL;
Ueberschwarz, Melbourne, AU; Arctic Paper Benelux.

**creative industries
fund NL**

ARCTIC PAPER

The editor and the publisher have made every effort
to secure permission to reproduce the listed material,
texts and illustrations. We apologize for any inadvert
errors or omissions. Parties who nevertheless believe
they can claim specific legal rights are invited to contact
the publisher. info@valiz.nl

This book has been produced with best-practice
methods ensuring lowest possible environmental
impact, using waterless offset, vegetable-based inks
and FSC-certified paper.

Amsterdam, 2016, second print 2019
ISBN 978-94-92095-19-0
NUR 656
Printed and bound in the EU